UP THE DOON

a television comedy in six parts

Andrew Neil

Dedicated to the inhabitants, past and present, of the Ayrshire villages of Patna, Mossblown and Annbank, and to the National Union of Mineworkers.

Although Patna and the Swallow pub actually exist, the characters and events in these plays are entirely fictitious.

First published in the United Kingdom in 2011
by Cut Yer Hair

ISBN 978–0–9570497–0–3

Produced by The Choir Press

Contents

Main Characters

ALEC GOURLAY – mid sixties. Retired coalminer.

SMILER FULTON – mid sixties. Retired coalminer.

WILMA GOURLAY – mid sixties. Canadian.

ISOBEL GOURLAY – early twenties. Canadian.

BETTY McNAB – mid sixties. B & B owner.

GEORGE McNAB – mid twenties. Unemployed.

BARBARA HYSLOP – early twenties. Barmaid.

OSWALD GRAY – early twenties. Student. African.

SINGER – early fifties. Musician, of sorts.

JINTY MUIR – mid sixties.

Episode One

EXT. AYR BEACH/LOW GREEN. AFTERNOON.
Alec and Smiler sitting wearing jackets, ties and bonnets, surrounded by holidaymakers soaking up the sun in swim wear.

SMILER See you?

ALEC Whit?

SMILER See if he's a twin?

ALEC He *is* a twin.

SMILER Aye, but see if he's an *identical* twin.

ALEC Whit?

SMILER It'll be like your birthday an' Christmas rolled intae one.

ALEC How come?

SMILER You can run up debts at the bookies, tell Ida Hyslop there's nae God, offer to shag Betty McNab – an' blame it all on him.

ALEC He's only here for a week!

SMILER What length of shag had you in mind?

ALEC [*not at all at ease*] What time is it?

Smiler shows him his watch.

ALEC Smiler, know something? I'm cakking myself. I'm sixty four an' this could be the most important day of my life.

SMILER You mean he could be rich?

ALEC Rich or poor, what does it matter? [*thinks –*] No! No, what am I saying? I take that back. But money's not what I'm talking about. [*spells it out –*] Separated when we were four. My mother buggers off to Canada with him and leaves me on a doorstep in Patna with a tin of condensed milk and a note that says, "Look after my wee boy, whoever you are, for I cannot afford to, and a new world beckons. Yours truly, anonymous. P.S. Excuse spelling ."

SMILER   And now the Sally Army computer's brought you together again after all these years.

ALEC   Aye, that's right. In about half an hour. The time's in his letter. Here's me – I'm gonna be standing in Ayr Station meetin' somebody called Wil I don't know from Adam, who's my own flesh and blood.

SMILER   You'll know certain things about him.

ALEC   Like what?

SMILER   He'll no' be an Ayr United supporter. He'll be in good company there. The bampots.

INT. AYR RAILWAY STATION. AFTERNOON.

Alec nervously watches passengers getting off a train, Smiler by his side. Eventually there is only a black man on the platform, and, a few yards further away, a woman with a suitcase. The black man walks towards them. Alec's jaw drops.

SMILER [*whispering*]   He could be your double, Alec. On a dark night, in a power cut, with the blinds drawn.

The man continues past them, heading for the taxi sign. Only the woman remains.

ALEC   He's only went and missed the bloody train!

SMILER   Hopes dashed, eh? The story of your life, Alec. Mind how we were wee and my mother used to take us to Woolworths for a Surprise Gift from Santa Claus and you hated jigsaws and your Surprise Gift was always a jigsaw? I bet this moment takes you back to them days.

The woman has come up. She taps on Alec's shoulder. He turns.

WOMAN   Is either of you Alexander, by any chance?

SMILER [*pointing*]   That'll be him.

WOMAN   I'm Wil.

ALEC   Wil??

WOMAN Wilma Gourlay. [*moved -*] I think I'm your sister.

ALEC [*gobsmacked*] In the name o' the wee man!

EXT. AYR BUS STOP. AFTERNOON.

The trio are about to board a bus. Alec, in a zombie-like trance, is about to step on. Smiler pulls him back.

SMILER [*indicating Wilma*] Ladies first!

Smiler ushers Wilma onto the bus. His newly-discovered etiquette hasn't quite matured to the point of carrying her suitcase.

INT. LIVING ROOM. LATE AFTERNOON.

Alec sits in his armchair, dazed. We hear a loo flush and jam and several attempts to get it working. Eventually –

ALEC [*calling off*] The handle's loose. Has been for years. Just wallop it up an' doon a few times. That usually does the trick.

Smiler appears from the kitchen carrying a tray set for three. Best china, but the milk bottle is slightly out of place.

SMILER I don't know when you last used the posh tea set, if ever, Alec, but wherever you got it from, you were robbed. Cracked saucers an' nae milk jug.

Wilma appears. Smiler enjoys a stab at grace.

Come away in, Wilma. Come into your brother's drawing room and have yir tea.

She joins Smiler on the sofa. Smiler holds out a plate.

Can I offer you a dod of cake? Spar's special.

WILMA Thank you.

She takes a slice. Smiler pours tea. They eat.

SMILER Happy families, eh?

Alec glares at him.

WILMA [*to Alec*] It's absolutely extraordinary. I have to keep pinching myself. I mean, I knew I had a twin, Mom told me that much, but she refused to talk about you. It was only when she died two years ago I was free to begin to search. It's been a nightmare trying to trace you.

SMILER I can imagine. Look at the size o' his feet. It'd take hours to trace them alone, forbye the rest of him.

WILMA Pardon?

ALEC Ignore him, he thinks he's funny.

SMILER You were saying, Wilma?

WILMA Well, I put adverts in newspapers, I advertised on the Internet, then, completely out of the blue, the Salvation Army computer in Toronto came up with a name and an address. No phone number, though.

ALEC [*a touch aggressive*] I don't believe in phones.

WILMA [*confused*] You don't *believe* in phones?

ALEC No, I don't.

SMILER [*an explanation for Wilma*] It's an expression. I don't believe in them either. And see them *mobile* phones? They're even worse. Years ago if you spotted someone walking down the street mumbling into the palm of their hand, it was because there was a can of Tennants in their fist. You knew where you were then, know what I mean?

She is lost. Smiler picks up the teapot.

Have another drap of tea. I'll be mother.

ALEC [*a contribution at last*] What was she like?

WILMA Domineering. Strict with me. Not so strict with herself. It was only on her death-bed she told me what had happened.

ALEC What did happen?

WILMA Well, she worked in an ice-rink kiosk in Ayr, and one day in her holidays she went on a "Mystery Coach Tour" to "the Trossachs", and during a stop for "tea and scones" she went for a walk in the woods and met the "Lord" or "Laird" who owned the land, and one thing led to another rather quickly, and she nearly missed the coach back. When she discovered she was pregnant, she tried to get in touch, but he didn't want to know.

SMILER [*disgusted*] Men! They're all the same!

ALEC Hang on! You once got Jinty Muir up the duff and denied it!

SMILER [*matter of fact*] That's what I'm saying : men – they're all the same.

ALEC [*to Wilma*] I can't.

WILMA Can't what?

ALEC I can't get my head round all this.

SMILER It's simple. This means you could be forty-something in line to the throne instead of forty eight million three hundred and fifty ninth. Conceived on your father's estate in the open air in a moment of unbridled passion between a Peer of the Realm and a woman who sold sweeties to skaters. You're half aristocrat, Alec.

He offers more cake to Wilma.

ALEC So what did "Mom" do?

WILMA She met a sailor. He wanted to take her home to Canada, but he couldn't cope with the two children. She took me, and left you behind.

SMILER Aye, on my mother's doorstep! Patna! She deliberately chose Patna! I mean, you don't just stumble on Patna! She must have really, really disliked you, Alec.

WILMA [*innocent*] What's so bad about Patna?

SMILER They were thinking about twinning Patna with Chernobyl, but Chernobyl said no way.

INT. B & B ROOM. EVENING.
Wilma, Alec and Smiler are inspecting the room. Mrs. McNab is inspecting Wilma.

MRS. MCNAB So, you're not from round here, you say?

WILMA No.

MRS. MCNAB Is that a touch of a Fife accent I can hear?

WILMA I'm from Canada.

MRS. MCNAB Canada? Whatever next?

ALEC I told you, Betty – she's my sister.

MRS. MCNAB [*officious*] I prefer "Mrs. McNab" when we're doing business, thank you very much. Sixty years you've lived in this village, Alec Gourlay. We went to school together, the three of us. I once knew you when you were a nice boy. It's a bit funny a sister nobody's ever heard of turning up. I dare say your house is like a midden and I can see why she wouldn't want to sleep there or even eat there, but let me tell you this : there'll be no hanky panky under my roof.

SMILER [*conciliatory*] C'mon, Betty . . . Mrs. McNab . . . this is well above board.

MRS. MCNAB [*fixing him with a glare*] I have only one thing to say to you, Smiler Fulton.

SMILER What's that, Mrs. McNab?

MRS. MCNAB Jinty Muir! [*to Wilma –*] How long will you be wanting the room for?

WILMA [*not unamused*] Only till Sunday morning.

MRS. MCNAB That's handy. My George is back on Monday and I need to get it ready for him.

SMILER [*mischief*] Does it take you long to pad the walls?

MRS. MCNAB I'll not have you talking like that, Smiler! [*to Wilma –*] My son's a bit . . . odd. In his head. But nothing serious, and not so's you'd notice. He sometimes goes away for a counselling thingy to help him get sorted out. Now, there's hangers in the wardrobe and a Bible in that drawer, and I've got a little dog – a poodle – and he'll be in and out and up and down, but he'll be no trouble to you, you won't even hear him. Not with the muzzle on.

EXT. HILLSIDE. AFTERNOON.
Alec, Wilma and Smiler are on a climb. Way below is the valley, the village, the river. They stop and survey.

ALEC You could see five pits from here.

WILMA Pits?

ALEC Coal mines. All gone. Patna's a ghost town now.

WILMA [*full of the view*] It's beautiful! And the river. Wow!

SMILER [*tourist guide*] That's the River Doon. Robert Burns? "Ye banks an' braes o' bonnie Doon."

ALEC It's not the river it was. Full of beer cans and used condoms in the good old days. When there were *young* men in the valley. Now it's Alzheimer Nursing Homes and long grass on the football pitch. Tell you what : there'll be nae mair Shankleys noo.

Wilma thinks : what language was that?

WILMA "Nay mayor shank lees new?"

ALEC [*repeating for her benefit*] There'll be nae mair Shankleys noo.

WILMA [*trying to get it*] "There'll be ... "

ALEC [*prompting*] Nae mair Shankleys noo.

WILMA [*slowly*] "There'll be nae mair Shankleys noo."

ALEC Very good. Near enough.

WILMA What does it mean?

ALEC It means no more wee men who couldnae spell "strategy" showing the world how to play football. It means no more pits, so no more putting your passion into controlling a leather ball to try to get out of them. It means a big dod of a certain kind of life oot the windae.

SMILER I'll tell you something, Alec : I don't know why the English were so bothered about getting a foreigner for a manager – that bloke Capello's in all likelihood slightly more intelligible than Shankley was.

WILMA [*to Alec*] I think I can see your house.

SMILER [*pointing*] There's mine as well, look. Just behind it.

WILMA [*peering*] Where?

SMILER Don't strain your eyes. They're all National Coal Board. Much of a muchness, really. The same architect, you see, would have designed the whole Housing Scheme while his guide-dog chased rabbits in the foothills.

They move on. Smiler nudges Wilma's arm.

SMILER [*ct'd*] Mind that sheep shite, hen. Excuse language.

ALEC [*to Wilma*] So you slept alright?

WILMA Fine, thanks.

ALEC What did she give you for breakfast?

WILMA A heaped plateful of things. Fried eggs. Toast. Beans. Spaghetti hoops. Black pudding. At least I think she called it black pudding.

ALEC Did you eat it?

WILMA I'm afraid not. I couldn't. Only the toast.

ALEC I'll get you a reduction on the bill if that's the story.

SMILER What Betty offered you was what her husband – Eddie – would have every morning without fail. In the days when he was eating. He's in the Alzheimers' Home now. Must be five years, eh, Alec? So Betty turns her house into a Bed and Breakfast. Like Patna was Blackpool. She even got pens made with the flags of all the EEC countries on them to give to visitors. And a sign saying, "Visa Cards Welcome". Betty McNab widnae know the difference between a Visa Card and a coal briquette. I think you're the first guest she's had.

They stop once more and look down and back.

WILMA [*a big exhalation*] Patna!

SMILER Patna, right enough. Also known as Mecca. Tae nobody.

WILMA [*joyous now*] My brother lives there! My twin brother!

A woman appears over the brow of the hill. As she draws level –

SMILER [*nodding in greeting*] Jinty.

JINTY [*nodding in greeting*] Smiler.

They watch as she walks on and away. Wilma glances at Smiler, who ignores her. As they head off for the top of the hill, Alec sings tunelessly and softly.

ALEC [*singing*] "Ye'll brek ma hert, ye warblin' bird, Wha sings sae blyhte abin the burn. Ye mind me o' departed joys, Departed never to return."

SMILER is not amused.

INT. THE "SWALLOW" PUB. EVENING.
Alec, Wilma and Smiler are sat with drinks. Wilma has had a few. She's not blootered, only tipsy, unused to the mix of whisky and heavy. At one end of the bar a self-styled singer is murdering a Jim Reeves number.

SINGER [*singing*] "Put your sweet lips a little closer, chew the phone ..." etc.

WILMA They don't have bars like this in Canada!

SMILER They don't have bars like this in Kilmarnock!

A woman [Ida] in outdoor clothes and clutching a Bible comes out from behind the bar, passing the barmaid [Barbara].

BARBARA See you later, mammy.

The woman nods. As she goes by Smiler's table on her way to the door –

SMILER Bit late for a Prayer Meeting, Ida.

IDA The Lord's clock is not man's clock.

SMILER Aye, right enough.

She goes. Two men are playing darts.

FIRST DART PLAYER [*as his third dart lands*] Ya beauty! One hundred and fifty seven!

The second darts player calculates the new score and chalks it up.

SMILER [*educating Wilma*] Witness the speed of the mathematics. Neither of them ever passed an exam at school, but see if they put their skill at calculating darts scores into the science of spaceflight? – Patna could have had a rocket on Mars by now. Same again, Wilma?

She nods after only a moment's hesitation.

ALEC It's my shout, Smiler.

SMILER I know it's your shout. I am well aware it's your shout. I was just making enquiries for you. Same again all round.

The singer comes over as Alec is about to go to the bar.

SINGER A pint o' heavy and a nippie sweetie for the entertainer, what d'you say, Alec?

ALEC An' what entertainer would that be?

Goes to the bar and calls back –

That's my sister from Canada. She's a big Jim Reeves fan. She thought you were performing some Gaelic folk-song.

SINGER [*shaking Wilma's hand*] Pleased to meet you, hen. How's it gon? Are you enjoyin' yourself?

WILMA I'm having a wonderful time, thank you.

SINGER [*sitting down*] What's your name?

WILMA Wil. Wilma.

SINGER Wilma? Would you credit it? Wilma was my mother's name. Is that not right, Smiler?

SMILER [*genuine surprise*] I never knew that.

SINGER Aye, it was Wilma, right enough. [*to Wilma –*] And do you know something? – this'll impress you till you hear the story – my mother answered the phone to Stanislavski!

WILMA [*all ears*] Stanislavski?

SINGER Sure thing. You see, Paddy Stratton, years ago, was the singer in this pub. He's dead now, but he used to sing here, and dress up and do turns at the Old Folks' Socials and such like, so everybody called him Stanislavsky, and one day my mother was comin' back from the shops and the phone was ringing in the phone box, and she went in, and here it was Stanislavsky ringing from the pit manager's office, hoping some passer-by would pick it up because he was just about to start on the back-shift and he'd left his sandwiches at home, and he wanted one of his boys to bring them over on the bike. So my mother picks it up and listens for a minute and says, "Is that you, Stanislavski?"

There is a knock on the door. Everybody stops what they're doing.

ALEC [*returning with drinks*] Is that somebody knocking? Who'd that be?

SMILER There's only one person stupid enough to knock on a pub door : George McNab.

BARBARA [*calling*] Come in, ya tube! But don't bring that dug wi' ye!

The door opens. George McNab stands there, holding an envelope. He spots Alec, darts across and hands it to him. Then the door closes and he's gone.

SMILER Who was that Masked Man on his silver charger? The Lone Ranger? No – the village idiot.

Alec opens the envelope. The letter is handwritten on lined notepaper.

ALEC [*reading*] "Dear Alec Gourlay, It is with deep regret that I have to inform you that my son George has come back early and is delivering this by hand."

SMILER Likely the shock treatment was pushing the counsellor's electricity bill through the roof.

ALEC "Therefore your sister – question mark, question mark – will have to find accomodation elsewhere, as we only have the two rooms unless George has a sleeping bag downstairs which is not advisable because of the dog. Your sister – question mark, question mark – owes £15 for one night's bed and breakfast – brackets, uneaten, close brackets. Visa cards welcome. Assuring you of our best attention at all times, yours truly, Betty McNab, Proprietor."

SMILER He must have come back this morning. It'd have taken Betty the best part of eight hours to write that.

ALEC What a bloody nuisance! If it's not one thing, it's another. Just when I thought I'd got the week sorted out. But don't you worry, Wilma. I'll have a think about where else you could stay. I mean, it's only five more nights.

WILMA [*getting attention*] Alec.

ALEC What?

WILMA I don't know how to say this.

ALEC You don't know how to say whit?

WILMA I think I want to stay.

ALEC What do you mean, you think you want to stay?

WILMA I think I might want to stay here for good.

SMILER [*eventually*] What one o' they words would it be that you don't understand, Alec? Would it be the long one?

ALEC is at sea. Everyone's looking at Wilma. She takes in her surroundings. She raises her glass. Slurring only slightly –

WILMA There'll be nae mair Shankleys noo!

INT. LIVING ROOM. EVENING.

WILMA is drinking coffee. Smiler is attacking a carry-out which occupies most of the table.

ALEC It's the drink talking, Wilma, honest it is. It's the drink's making you rash.

WILMA Don't you like me?

ALEC Of course I like you! Don't be stupid. How could I not like you?

WILMA Am I your sister?

ALEC Of course you're my sister! – my mother left my birth certificate in the condensed milk tin. What is this – "Who Wants To Be A Millionaire?"

WILMA Aren't you lonely? Even a little bit?

ALEC Lonely! Lonely? Lonely's for TV documentaries. Lonely's for Vera Lynn songs and pub karaoke.

SMILER [*drunk, and a touch behind*] So that's what the pair of skates was!

ALEC What pair of skates? What are you on about?

SMILER My mother said when she opened the door, you were standing there with a note and a tin of condensed milk in one hand, and a pair of skates in the other! And Wilma said yesterday your mother worked in an ice-rink. It was your mother leaving you a wee bit of herself!

WILMA [*asking Smiler*] What happened to them?

SMILER We threw them away. They were junk.

ALEC [*back to business*] Look, this is only your second day here. You've got a distorted impresion of Patna.

SMILER It's been dry for a start.

ALEC [*clutching at straws*] That's right! Two days without rain! Records are being broken! I've never seen a pair of sun glasses in the Doon Valley.

SMILER [*prompting*] The Minister.

ALEC Except when the Minister fell off the ladder watching you having foreplay with Jinty Muir in the alley by the manse and was trying to hide his black eye in the Church that Sunday.

SMILER Whit's foreplay?

WILMA [*she means it*] Listen, Alec, I'll not stay if I'm not welcome.

ALEC It's not that, it's just …

WILMA Just what?

ALEC In the name o' the wee man! I'm nearly sixty five! I'm settled in my ways! It's been great to meet you, and everything, really great, and to know I've got a family – well, *you* – but I imagined we'd have a sort of trans Atlantic relationship. Christmas cards, that kind of stuff. You maybe coming here for the odd short holiday.

WILMA Letters across the ocean?

ALEC The post's very good here. I'd even get the phone in.

Wilma gets up.

ALEC [*alarmed*] What's up? Where are you going?

WILMA I need to powder my nose.

SMILER That'll be Canadian for having a pish, then?

WILMA goes to the loo. Smiler pours himself more drink.

Maybe you should move to Canada, Alec.

ALEC Get tae! Don't talk pish! I couldnae do that.

SMILER Why not?

ALEC I'd miss things.

SMILER What would you miss, but?

They're looking at each other.

ALEC I don't know. Things.

We hear the loo flush and jam. Alec calls off instinctively.

The bloody handle's loose!

WILMA [*off*] I know. Just wallop it up and doon a few times. That usually does the trick.

SMILER Did you hear that? The polish of that sentence? She could be Patna born and bred.

INT. BEDROOM. MIDNIGHT.

Wilma is tucked up in bed. Alec, still dressed, is perched on the edge. The clock chimes.

WILMA Are you sure you'll be alright on the chair in the drawing room?

ALEC I'll be fine.

WILMA And we'll talk in the morning? Yes?

ALEC We'll talk in the morning. Is the bed O.K?

WILMA It's fine. Very comfortable.

ALEC Not too lumpy?

She shakes her head.

And you know how to switch the electric blanket on if you need it?

She nods.

And the glass for your teeth's just down by my feet here.

She nods again.

WILMA I'm O.K. to have a bath in the morning – yes?

ALEC [*surprised*] A bath? O? Aye, aye. I'll remember to put the water on before I go to sleep. I usually have mine on a Monday, you see. Force of habit. About what time are you thinkin' you'll be having your bath?

WILMA As soon as I wake up. Is that a problem?

ALEC No. No. Listen, do you have any memories at all of our life before you went to Canada?

WILMA Not really. Why?

ALEC Well, I think we must have stayed in Mossblown, about fifteen miles from here, somewhere like that, miners' rows without inside water. I can remember the toilet was in a kind of field outside, and if you had to go during the night, it was hellish. It was alright if it was just a pee, for there was a bucket by the door, but, as can only be expected, sometimes it wasn't a pee you wanted, and then you had to wake this woman up – my mother, *our* mother, I suppose – and she hated you for it. She had to get a torch and take you across to this toilet in the field – a wooden thing about the size of a phone box – and wait while you did your business. And every five seconds or so she'd be yelling, "Have you finished yet?" because, naturally, she wanted to get back to her kip, you see.

WILMA [*listening hard*] I don't remember anything like that.

ALEC No, well, maybe you don't, but the point is, now that I've got my own toilet, an' my own *freedom*, so to speak, to make up for the early days, the bad days, I'm in there for at least an hour of a morning. I take the wireless in. I take a paper in. I take my breakfast in. Know what I'm trying to say?

She nods, full of warmth.

By the way, there's a very sturdy loo brush in there for when some bits stick to the bowl.

He rises, awkward, not knowing how to finish it.

Well, I'll say goodnight.

WILMA [*so warm*] Goodnight, brother.

ALEC [*softly*] Goodnight, sister.

He starts to go.

WILMA Alec?

She holds her face up. He waits, unsure, then leans down and kisses her cheek. He suddenly pulls away.

ALEC You nearly made me knock your teeth glass over!

As he closes the door –

WILMA Sweet dreams!

INT. LIVING ROOM. MIDDLE OF THE NIGHT.
We hear the dawn chorus. Alec is in the armchair, exhausted, staring straight ahead, a blanket round him.

ALEC Listen, I don't know if there's anybody there or not, but if there is, this is Alec Gourlay talking tae you from Patna. I don't suppose you remember making Patna, you were likely rat-arsed at the time.

He listens for a reply.

If it'd be easier for you if I was on my knees, just give me a sign.

No sign arrives.

I haven't been on my knees for years. Not since I caught Jinty Muir on the rebound from Smiler. I'm in the horns of a dilema, big boy. That's why I'm yappin' to you. I bet it's the only time you get a wee bit of conversation : when folk are in some kinda crisis – a puncture on their bike, a homing pigeon that doesn't come home, that sorta thing. Well, to put you fully in the picture, in case you've had your hands full in Ethiopia, or Dalrymple or somewhere, I've got my newly-discovered twin sister here, and she wants to emigrate. To Patna.

Imagines the reaction.

No, she's no' aff her heid that you can tell. I mean, she's a nice enough woman, but she's a woman for a start. I've never had a woman in the house except for that new doctor when I had to have they enemas.

He tries reasoning.

You're like me : you're on your tod as well up there. How would you feel if Mary or Ruth or one o' that lot wanted to move in wi' you? I mean, Heaven's a big place, and them being the equivalent of an ocean away's fine, but I bet if any one of them suggested moving into your actual *hoose*, you'd be tellin' them where to get off, smartish. This hoose is no' big enough. I don't even know if she can cook.

He begins to drift off.

ALEC [*ct'd*] What a palaver! Maybe if I play a lotta Jimmy Shand records, that'll change her mind. "The Bluebell Polka" on a loop – that could be the answer.

The dawn chorus comes up in volume.

They birds out there have it easy. Lucky as anything. Don't even know they were born.

A long sigh.

Ahhh … I wish I had never evolved. In the name o' the wee man …

And he's asleep.

Episode Two

INT. THE "SWALLOW" PUB. MORNING.

Barbara has just opened up and is laying out beer mats. There's a knock on the door.

BARBARA [*sighing*] It's open, ya ijit! I've just unlocked it!

Another knock.

Push, ya dummy! Are you pulling again? An' leave that scabby poodle outside, mind!

The door opens and it's Wilma.

I beg your pardon. I thought it was George McNab with this morning's paper. What can I get you?

WILMA Do you do coffee?

BARBARA I've been asked for all sorts of things in here, including Duraglit squeezed out and mixed with cider, but I don't remember ever being asked for coffee, or a soft drink of any kind, in fact. I'll stick the kettle on through the back, if you don't mind waiting.

Wilma nods. Barbara exits. Wilma sits apprehensively. Barbara returns.

You're not local, are you? Are you . . . ?

WILMA I've been here for less than a week. I'm Alec Gourlay's sister.

BARBARA O aye, that's right. His twin. You were in here the other night. How do you like Patna, then?

WILMA It's lovely. Patna's great.

BARBARA You haven't just arrived from a lifetime in a Siberian gulag, by any chance?

WILMA smiles, beginning to get used to the local humour.

WILMA No. Actually, I've come to ask a favour. I wonder if I could use your telephone. The public kiosk doesn't seem to be working.

BARBARA Vandalised during the celebrations for Charles and Diana's wedding.

WILMA I'd pay, of course.

BARBARA Sure. Nae problem. It's through the back here.

She lifts the bar flap.

WILMA It is long-distance.

BARBARA Kilmarnock – that sort of area?

WILMA Canada. I have a rather important phone call to make to my daughter.

BARBARA So Alec's got a niece, then. That's nice for him.

Wilma is about to go into the corridor.

WILMA It would be if he knew.

As Barbara shows surprise, there's a knock on the door again. Barbara yells as she ushers Wilma towards the phone.

BARBARA Push, ya lunatic! And that dug's barred!

EXT. MAIN STREET. MORNING.

Alec and Smiler are walking up from the stone bridge. George McNab cycles past. Barking noises come from a carrier on his bike.

SMILER Maybe Betty dropped him on his head soon after he was born. I'm surprised he's no' managing Ayr United.

ALEC Where the hell can she be, Smiler?

SMILER Probably drowned. Floatin' face-down in the Doon round about Dalmellington.

ALEC It's not funny! Anyway, Dalmellington's upstream.

SMILER She said she was going for a walk, for Heaven's sake.

ALEC But on her own! Why would she want to go for a walk on her own?

SMILER Maybe she wanted to go to the toilet.

ALEC There's a perfectly good toilet in ma hoose!

SMILER Aye, but you'd just been in there. It's a wise man, or woman, who gives it an hour or so to clear.

They pause for breath. Smiler looks over the manse wall.

Would you credit the Minister's garden? Not a leaf, not a blade of grass out of place. It'll be him being on the one-day-week explains the prize-winning nature of his landscaping.

The singer comes round the corner, jogging in a track-suit.

SINGER [*through wheezes*] 'Mornin', boys. Dalrymple karaoke on Saturday. It's a competition this week. I fancy ma chances. Jimmy Milby's gonna be there, who used to be Overman at the Big Mine at Pennyvenie for a while. Remember Jimmy? Used to win the Slow Bicycle race at New Cumnock regularly. When the pits shut, he did singing gigs at Sundrham Holiday Park until the night he sang, "O, Mr. Fisherman" and there were weans in the audience. Well, Jimmy's gonna be at Dalrymple right enough, but I figure if I keep up the training I'll have the edge on him, especially seein' as his emphysema's a lot worse than mine is.

He jogs off, trying to hold a tune.

"Doctor Macgregor and his wee black bag,
Doctor Macgregor and his wee black bag,
He's known at every cottage door
Through all the countryside,
There's not a bed in all the place He hasn't sat beside,
The ladies all adore him,
Though he's never one to brag :
They're glad to see Macgregor
And his wee black bag."

He's out of earshot, and Alec and Smiler have reached the McNab B & B, where George is in the garden casting a fishing-rod. They watch him for a few moments.

SMILER What kind o' fish is it you'd be catchin' there, George? Would it be shoals? Or just the single fish?

A dog barks inside the house. Betty appears at an upstairs window.

BETTY You leave my wee boy alone, Smiler Fulton!

SMILER   Just passing the time o' day, Betty. Just making conversation.

BETTY Well, don't! And as for you, Alec Gourlay, I've only got one thing to say to you.

ALEC What's that, Betty?

She mimes drinking.

Whit?

Again she mimes drinking.

Is there some Marcel Marceau competition coming up that I haven't heard of?

She closes the window, but from behind it once more raises an imaginary glass mysteriously to her lips. Smiler absorbs this, and the fishing, and the barking dog.

SMILER It's hereditary. It's in the genes. No question.

ALEC Where can she be, Smiler?

INT. LIVING ROOM. LATE MORNING.
Alec and Smiler are there. Wilma has arrived moments ago. Alec is furious.

ALEC The Swallow! You went into the Swallow at a minute past eleven! Not just Betty McNab, they'll *all* be thinkin' my sister's an alkie!

WILMA I only had a coffee.

ALEC They don't sell coffee in the Swallow! They don't even sell crisps in the Swallow! That's why it's called the Swallow! You go in there to swallow ethyl alcohol in one form or another! Not for sandwiches! Not for musak! You go in there to buy drink that makes you pished!

SMILER Hold on! We're not talking "Judgement At Nuremberg" here.

ALEC [*to Smiler*] You shut yir face! [*to Wilma –*] There's instant coffee in the kitchen. There's even a bottle of Camp in a cupboard somewhere, and you don't even need to add sugar to that. As a matter of fact, you could live in this house without ever having to step out of the front door, given that there's an Indian take-away in the Main Street, and they deliver.

SMILER Not having a phone in the house, would it be a pigeon that delivered your Venison Tikka Masala order?

ALEC I told you to keep yir mooth shut!

He pulls himself together to explain.

I just don't want to be anything less than a perfect host. You're likely not here for long, and I don't want it not to be smooth. Now, do you fancy a cup of tea, or a wee glass of port, or something?

SMILER That'll be the "sun's just gone over the yard-arm" wee glass of port, will it?

ALEC is about to get angry again.

WILMA [*taking control*] Listen. Listen, yes I did go to the Swallow, and, yes, I did have a cup of coffee, but there was something else I had to do that was very, very important, and you need to know about it, Alec. You need to know what it was. And I think you ought to be sitting down to hear it.

What on earth is this? Alec sits. Smiler leans forward formally to receive whatever news is about to be delivered. Wilma looks from one to the other and loses her bottle.

But first I have to use the toilet.

She exits rather quickly.

ALEC Whatever next?

SMILER A pish, I would imagine. At least her knickers'll only be round her ankles. Yours are in a right twist. I don't think I've ever seen you so rattled. Not since you were told last year you had to have some enemas, an' saw the length o' the tube.

ALEC Well, what do you expect?

SMILER The lassie only went for a coffee.

ALEC It's not the coffee.

SMILER Well, what is it, but?

ALEC Everything. How long is she staying for. Stuff like that.

SMILER So you've not decided?

ALEC Naw.

SMILER How no'?

ALEC Because I need time to think, that's how no'! It's an awfy, awfy big decision, somebody movin' in here.

SMILER She's not just somebody. She's your sister.

ALEC She's still somebody.

SMILER I think we just hit a wee cul de sac of logic there.

ALEC And this something else that's "very, very important". What's that likely to be?

SMILER Alec, there are two things I am not. One is an Ayr United supporter. Two is a medium.

There is the noise of the loo sticking.

ALEC You have to wallop the handle up and doon a few times!

WILMA [*entering*] I know.

She resumes her seat. They wait.

I'd rather neither of you went in there just yet.

SMILER [*to Alec*] It's in the genes. No question.

Alec glares. They wait.

ALEC [*to Wilma*] I'm sitting.

But her bottle has gone.

WILMA Well, it's a woman's thing. A female thing.

ALEC [*lost*] A "woman's thing"?

WILMA The barmaid's a woman. I talked to her. I knew she'd know. [*clutching at straws*] Where to buy … something. She said Ayr. I should go to Ayr.

ALEC [*still lost*] A "woman's thing"?

SMILER Leave it, Alec. Just like racing pigeons and chewing tobacco are men's things, so certain things are woman's things.

ALEC Jinty Muir's mother.

SMILER Jinty Muir's mother whit?

ALEC Jinty Muir's mother chewed tobacco.

SMILER Alec. Alec, that Jinty Muir's mother chewed tobacco is not the point!

EXT. AYR SEA-FRONT. AFTERNOON.
Wilma and Smiler are sitting in a shelter looking across the water. Silence until Smiler indicates a carving on the wall.

SMILER See this shelter?

WILMA Yes.

SMILER Guess whit age it is.

WILMA [*not fully engaged*] I have no idea.

SMILER This shelter has been here since Roman times.

She shakes her head in disbelief.

It's a fact. An' I can prove it. See that there on the wall? Somebody's carved, "Ayr United for the Cup", well, naebody since the Romans would have been stupid enough to dae that.

She's still distant. A flock of seagulls screeches overhead.

Look at they gulls arseing about. Do you think they make that noise deliberately, or is it just the wind catching in their throats? [*no response*] I mean, is it like bees putting their lips together to make that buzzing sound to let you know they're coming?

WILMA The sound that bees make is produced by the speed of the action of their wings.

SMILER Get away wi' you! Is that right? Fair enough. You learn something every day. Just as well I never had my sight set on being an animal scientist, isn't it?

He's not getting through.

Look, listen, I'm sorry. I know you insisted you wanted to come into Ayr by yourself, and I'm sorry I sneaked onto the bus at the stop at the bottom of the Scheme, I shouldn't have done that, but I was worried you might get lost. Ayr's a big place compared to

Patna. It's like if Patna [*searches*], if Patna was the varicose vein, Ayr would be the whole leg. Anyway, please accept my apologies. I'll away back to the bus station and leave you to buy whatever it is you have to buy, and find your own way hame.

WILMA "Hame"?

SMILER [*thinking she needs a translation*] "Home ."

WILMA Is Patna my home?

SMILER [*confused*] I mean, find your own way back to Alec's hoose.

WILMA Is "Alec's hoose" my home now, Smiler?

SMILER [*a bit too deep for him*] Well, you two are talking that through, aren't you?

WILMA I can't go back, Smiler.

SMILER What do you mean, you can't go back? There's a bus every half hour. Just try to get one that goes direct, not the one that goes through Dalrymple. I don't think you're strong enough yet for Dalrymple. I don't think anyone's strong enough yet for Dalrymple.

WILMA No, I can't go back to Canada.

SMILER [*very surprised, then logical*] Nae money?

WILMA O, I've got the money.

SMILER How not, then?

WILMA My daughter ...

She waits, knowing he has to say something.

SMILER That'll be the one you've never mentioned.

WILMA [*nodding*] My daughter works in government in Edmonton in Canada. She stumbled on a fraud. On a fairly large scale. She was incensed, naturally, but her hands were tied. If she leaked the information she'd lose her job, her career, everything, almost. So I leaked it instead. They'd be able to make life very, very difficult if I returned. I rang my daughter from the Swallow this morning to see how things were. I lied about why I had to come to Ayr. I wanted time to think. On my own.

A long wait while he thinks.

SMILER So you're a kind of whistle-blower? [*she nods*] As long as you're not a referee, that's alright, I suppose. I suppose you're a kind of heroine. A've never met a heroine before. That was a very [*searches*] swashbuckling kind of thing ye did back in Canada.

She looks slightly taken aback. He notices.

"Swashbuckling." It sounds right for what ye did. Aye. "Swashbuckling." I heard it in a film. Nae idea whit it means.

A woman walks past the entrance to the shelter. She looks in. Smiler nods in greeting.

Jinty.

JINTY [*nodding in greeting*] Smiler.

Jinty walks out of sight. Wilma looks at Smiler, who ignores her.

EXT. PATNA BUS STOP. LATE AFTERNOON.

ALEC is scanning the road impatiently. Barbara approaches.

BARBARA So, you'll not be going to Dalmellington, then, Alec?

ALEC No.

BARBARA I thought as much. You've let four buses go past.

ALEC I'm waitin' for somebody.

BARBARA Same here. Do you want to know who it is?

ALEC Naw. I don't care who it is.

BARBARA I could be waiting for Mel Gibson.

ALEC If he uses the same accent he used in "Braveheart", I've no doubt he'll be on the wrang bus.

BARBARA No. I'm waiting for my boyfriend. We met at University. He's from England. He's coming for some of the University holidays.

ALEC What size shoes does he take?

BARBARA Nine. Why do you ask?

ALEC I'm just trying to show you I'm not in the least bit interested in who you're waitin' for or why you're waitin' for them.

BARBARA You're sometimes a crabbit old bastard, Alec Gourlay, do you know that? I thought you'd be makin' some kind of effort, with your sister visiting.

ALEC You leave my sister out of this.

BARBARA God knows whit your niece'll think.

ALEC I hivnae got a niece.

BARBARA You hiv tae.

ALEC I hiv not.

BARBARA Please yersel'.

ALEC [*eventually*] Whit made you say I've got a niece? Eh? Whit?

BARBARA Well, I drew some air intae my lungs and expelled it by way of my vocal chords while forming consonontal and vowel patterns with my lips and tongue, and – would you believe it? – oot it came.

ALEC Don't give me that clever University stuff, just tell me why you said I had a niece.

BARBARA I'm a medium.

ALEC You're no' a medium, you're a scunner, that's whit you are! An' you're manky at pullin' pints as well. The sooner you go back tae University the better.

Barbara is grinning.

Do you know somethin' I don't?

Barbara winks and puts a finger to her lips.

I hope your boyfriend gets eczema aff the bus seat!

INT. ON THE BUS. LATE AFTERNOON.
Wilma and Smiler travelling on the back seat.

SMILER You can open your eyes now – we're through Dalrymple.

She opens them.

The only way you can cope with Dalrymple is if you're steamin' drunk. If God wanted to give the world an enema, that's where he'd put the tube, right enough.

Wilma is taking in the scenery. At the front of the bus is Oswald, who is black. Smiler points to him and whispers.

SMILER [*ct'd*] I wonder if he's headin' for Patna. That'd be a turn up for the books. The last time there was a black man in Patna was the day they lost the key to the pit baths in 1957.

WILMA Were you a miner all your life?

SMILER Not before I was fourteen.

WILMA What was being a coal miner like?

SMILER Just a job.

WILMA Was your father a miner?

SMILER Aye. An' his. An' his.

WILMA Is it what you wanted to be?

SMILER Nae choice, really. When I was wee, I wanted to be a cowboy. I once wrote to Hopalong Cassidy and asked him if he had any old guns he didn't use anymore. Have they got cowboys in Canada?

WILMA A long time ago.

SMILER They even had women cowboys in the Wild West, didn't they? That Jessie James, for example.

WILMA Jesse James was a man.

SMILER Is that right? Wi' a name like that? Was he gay, do you think?

WILMA Who knows? I wondered for a very, very little while whether you might be.

SMILER [*astounded*] Me!? Gay?? I enjoy a laugh, but "gay" gay?? Whatever put that intae your heid?

WILMA You and Alec are inseperable.

SMILER We grew up together, for Heaven's sake! Since we were four! Since his mother abandoned him on my mother's doorstep without so much as a by your leave and swanned off to Canada with you. I know you said her fancy man couldn't stand Alec, but there must have been another reason she dumped him, and, knowing him, very likely it was because he was still wantin' to breast-feed! Gay!! I've never heard anythin' so silly in my life!

WILMA As I say, it was a thought that came and went in seconds.

Wilma takes in the scenery again. Smiler is thinking hard.

SMILER Has anyone ever proposed marriage to you on a Dalmellington bus?

WILMA [*did she hear this?*] What?

SMILER Well, I'm thinking about it.

WILMA Don't be silly, Smiler.

SMILER Not so silly as you've just been being. Gay. Me. Do you know somethin'? If we'd caught the direct bus an' not done the detour through Dalrymple, we'd have been in Patna fifteen minutes ago, an' none of this conversation would have taken place. Some rogue nation should nuke Dalrymple. I've always thought that.

INT. LIVING ROOM. LATE AFTERNOON.
Wilma and Smiler are sitting with cups of tea. Alec is in a complete huff in the armchair.

SMILER Have you taken a vow of silence, or what? The woman here's trying to have a reasonable conversation with you, an' you're behaving like a slab o' concrete or an Ayr United goalkeeper. She pulled the plug on some fraud, so she did. It's no' as if she was a hit man for the Mafia.

ALEC [*sullen*] It's not that.

WILMA What is it, then?

ALEC [*to Wilma*] Everybody in Patna seems to know all about you before I do.

SMILER [*mimicing*] "Everybody in Patna seems to know all about you before I do." Honestly, Alec, you're like an old woman some-times.

But the bus conversation jumps into mind and he darts a glance to Wilma.

Forget I said that! Just forget it! Right?

ALEC So I've got a niece.

WILMA Yes.

ALEC Anything else you're hiding from me?

WILMA No.

ALEC Has she got a name?

WILMA Isobel.

SMILER That's nice.

WILMA She's twenty three. I was in my early forties when I had her. Her father and I never married.

SMILER In the genes, you see.

WILMA He left when Isobel was months old. One of the reasons he left was because he couldn't stand my – our – mother. But there were other reasons. He wasn't what you'd call a gentleman, really.

SMILER [*still contributing redundantly*] In Patna the definition of a gentleman is somebody who gets out of the bath to pee.

ALEC Smiler, will you shut yir trap, will you?

WILMA When I spoke to her on the telephone this morning, she said to say hello.

   Alec calls, as if to Canada.

ALEC Hello!

   We're all waiting for Alec's next move.

What I can't understand, what I can't get ma heid roon, is that she cannae give this story to the papers because of the come-back, so you give it, then abscond to Patna to avoid the flak, but you're her mother, and as soon as the guilty parties read the story, unless they're McNabs, they'll put two and two together and make four and realise that who you got the information from is her.

WILMA You're right.

ALEC Whit do you mean I'm right?

WILMA We, naively, didn't think they would, but that's exactly what they did.

ALEC So?

WILMA So now Isobel's in a bit of trouble. We need to sort it out.

ALEC "We"?

WILMA Her and me.

ALEC Ah. So you're flying back?

WILMA No. She's flying here.

INT. THE "SWALLOW" PUB. EVENING.

Alec, Smiler and Oswald are at a table drinking. Barbara is serving behind the bar.

SMILER Oswald *Grey* did Barbara say your name was?

OSWALD That's right.

SMILER Fair enough.

OSWALD I'm a great fan of Robert Burns.

SMILER The Whiteletts Robert Burns? Makes the best ice cream in Ayrshire. See they oysters wi' the coconut in the middle? Magic, them.

OSWALD Robert Burns, the poet.

SMILER O, him. He's deid. Him that farmed in Alloway? Hung about the Masonic Lodge in Tarbolton? Got a few Mauchline lassies pregnant?

OSWALD Yup.

SMILER Imagine gettin' anybody from Mauchline pregnant. It'd be like eatin' in a restaurant in Dalrymple. If there was one. Oswald, I keep thinking I've seen you before.

ALEC It's when the pits were still open. Everybody looked like Oswald then. Imagine him lyin' on his side takin' a pick to a twenty seven inch seam at the bottom of the Big Mine at Dalmellington. Could be any Patna man you care to name.

He's had his eye on the bar.

Barbara, would you be free now to give yourself a break and come and join us?

BARBARA Your sister's changing you, Alec Gourlay. You actually asked me that as if I was a human being.

She comes over and sits, holding hands with Oswald.

ALEC Whit age are you?

BARBARA I'll be twenty three next month.

ALEC What would make you like me?

BARBARA I already like you, Alec. Have you been drinkin' at hame? Are you pished?

ALEC I'm no' pished. I just want tae know the sort of things I could do that would make you like me. Really like me?

BARBARA [*to Smiler*] Is this a wind-up?

SMILER I have absolutely no idea where he is going with this, or why, Barbara. The man's mind of late is even more a mystery than before. It might be the first seeds of dementia, who knows? I personally put it down to having to sit with himself in the toilet of a morning, with the door shut.

ALEC I'm serious.

BARBARA Things to do that would make me like you?

ALEC Really, really like me. Things I could give you.

BARBARA Are you talking about buying me presents, Alec Gourlay?

ALEC It's a hypothesis.

SMILER Is a hypothesis one o' they things Pythagoras worked out? [*then the penny drops*] Or are you talking about your niece?

BARBARA O, I get it. You've never met your niece, and she's about my age. You want me to give you a list of really nice, thoughtful presents, and you'll get them for her. Is that it?

ALEC Nearly.

BARBARA How d'you mean "nearly"?

ALEC I mean, I'll get the opposite.

INT. LIVING ROOM. LATE EVENING.

Alec and Wilma are sitting down to a meal which Wilma has prepared.

ALEC No, no! You put the vinegar on first, or it just washes the salt off. I've seen meals sent back for that very reason.

WILMA I'm learning something new every day.

ALEC Every day? Don't talk about every day! There's bigger things happened here in the last seven days than in the last twenty seven years.

WILMA What happened twenty seven years ago?

ALEC Well, there was the Miners' Strike twenty seven years ago, an' there was the day five years ago the McNab poodle took a big lump out the Minister's leg. Things have been quiet since then, what wi' the miners losing an' the poodle gettin' muzzled. Then you turn up. Gonnae pass the brown sauce?

She does. They are eating.

When did you say Isobel was thinkin' of comin' for your discussions?

WILMA Next month is the earliest she can get away. About four weeks time.

ALEC An' you're sure it's not somethin' you can do over the phone?

WILMA No, it'll need a little time, face to face.

ALEC What's the postal system like in Canada?

WILMA In what way?

ALEC Would it be modern, quite efficient?

WILMA Of course. Why do you ask?

ALEC Well, as I'm her only uncle and stuff, I was thinking I might send her a wee gift, just to say hello from across the ocean.

WILMA [*touched*]   You're a nice, nice man, Alec Gourlay, underneath all that rough exterior.

ALEC Aye. [*pause*] Whit rough exterior?

She just smiles. They continue to eat.

WILMA So, what does this mean?

ALEC What does whit mean?

WILMA You're talking about next month as though I'm still going to be living here. Are you trying to tell me something?

ALEC Do you want to be still living here next month?

WILMA [*simply*] Yes.

ALEC Well, I guess that's alright by me.

A huge moment. She goes to kiss him, but he holds his hand up.

I wisnae sure at first. I mean, it's a wee hoose, and I'm used to havin' it to myself, but you're ma sister, an' all our lives we've been apart, but now we've met up, an' I like you, I really, really like you, and we're neither of us young, an' maybe it's right we end up together like this before the Man Wi' The Big Scythe gives us a shout.

It's as important a statement as he's ever made in his life. She leans over, but again he stops her.

But. I can't sleep on the armchair forever, so we'll need to buy a foldable Z-bed for in here, an' you can have the bedroom one week an' I'll have it the next. An' we'll need tae get a few more plates an' cups an' things, an' don't ever be tempted to open the bottle of sherry under the sink, for I won it in a raffle years ago an' I think it'd rot your guts now. *Plus*, bagsy me first in the toilet of a morning. Agreed?

This time he lets her kiss him. A magical atmosphere as they both realise what's been done. As she rises to clear up –

WILMA I should tell you that Smiler proposed to me today on the bus coming home.

ALEC Would that be just after you went through Dalrymple?

WILMA Uh huh.

ALEC Ignore anything that happens within a five mile radius of Dalrymple. Anythin' at all. Fancy a tatty scone with sugar on it?

And he waits for an answer.

Episode Three

INT. THE "SWALLOW" PUB. LATE MORNING.

Singer is tuning his guitar. Isobel, with a suitcase, is sitting at a table. Barbara comes from behind the bar with a coffee.

BARBARA [*to Singer*] Gonnae give that a rest, will you? It would cut yir hair.

SINGER [*can't hear*] Whit?

BARBARA [*shouting*] I said, gonnae pack that racket in?

SINGER [*pausing*] I'm tunin' my guitar. I have tae tune it for my recital tonight. I could do wi' another pint o' heavy as well.

BABBARA If I get you another pint, gonnae rest that noise for a wee while?

SINGER I suppose I could finish my poster.

BARBARA [*calling*] Oswald!

Oswald appears behind the bar.

Darlin', would you mind getting a pint o' heavy for Django Reinhart here? And put it on the tab. That's his fourth this morning.

Oswald pulls a pint. Singer gets his crayons out and spreads his poster on the table. Barbara joins Isobel, handing her the coffee.

I'm sorry we haven't got real coffee, hen.

SINGER What's that, then? Imaginary coffee?

BARBARA You'll get an imaginary bat on the mooth if you don't mind your ain business. [*to Isobel –*] Is it O.K?

ISOBEL [*sipping and lying*] Fine, thanks.

BARBARA They probably went out for the day. That's it, I would think.

ISOBEL My flight got put forward by twenty four hours. I had no way of getting in touch.

BARBARA You're welcome to stay here an' keep your eye on the buses. They'll get off at the stop along the road. Unless, which is highly unlikely, they catch a Dalrymple bus that goes up the Scheme.

SINGER I was in the Dalrymple Karaoke Competition last month, so I was. Came second. Close thing. Neck and neck for a while. Me an' Jimmy Milby. Overman at the Big Mine at Dalmellington before it shut. He's only got the one lung now. It was nearly a draw, but. Have you heard o' Jimmy?

BARBARA What do you mean, has she heard o' Jimmy? She's just flew in from Canada, ya bampot.

SINGER But I think Jimmy's got relatives in Canada.

BARBARA [*to Isobel*] Don't despair, hen. There is intelligent life in Patna. Mind you, it's on the hills, covered in wool, chewing grass.

EXT. MOSSBLOWN. LATE MORNING.

Alec, Wilma and Smiler are standing on the bridge, looking down on the railway line and the village.

SMILER There it is : Mossblown!

WILMA Mossblown. How did it come by its name?

SMILER No idea. Probably named by some land-owning aristo-crat with a poetic imagination and extremely bad eyesight.

ALEC [*to Wilma*]   I wanted you to see it, even if just the once.

WILMA Because you think we may have been born here?

ALEC That's Smiler's theory.

SMILER Well, here, but inside. I mean, it was primitive, but the actual birth would have been indoors.

WILMA You were definitely born here, Smiler, were you?

SMILER Absolutely. 71, Long Row, Mossblown. Long Row. Imaginatively named because all the way down there, by the side of the railway line, where them modern houses are now, there was a long row of miners' hooses. We moved tae Patna when my father changed pits when I was two. I think you two must have lived here, an' when your mother decided to abandon Alec an' whip you off to Canada, she nipped up tae Patna an' dumped him on our doorstep, where my mother fell over him when she was takin' the rubbish out.

WILMA Where was the pit?

SMILER   There was Mossblown Mine over there. Annbank Number Nine back there. An a' the rest.

ALEC You couldnae move for coal in Ayrshire. It's still there. It's just that naebody wants it now.

WILMA [*to Smiler*] Would your parents have owned their house?

SMILER Don't be daft, hen. A two-room affair with no inside water an' no inside toilet, owned by the National Coal Board. Rented. Same as now.

ALEC I'm just standin' here thinkin'. I've never owned anythin' in my life bigger than you could put intae a big suitcase.

SMILER Whit about that table in your living room?

ALEC O, aye. Right enough. Shall we get started back?

WILMA In a moment. I just want to stand here for a moment.

They stand, looking.

ALEC [*to Wilma*] Penny for your thoughts.

WILMA O, this and that. Mossblown. Patna. You. Me. Isobel.

ALEC Nothing to worry about as far as Isobel is concerned. I've checked the times of trains to Glasgow, an' how long it'll take to get to the airport from the railway station. I'll set the alarm for plenty of time in the morning.

SMILER You owe Wilma a penny, by the way.

ALEC [*ignoring him*] An' we can have an Indian take-away tomorrow night. Bit of a celebration.

WILMA Isobel's a vegetarian, I'm afraid.

ALEC She's a what?

WILMA She's a vegetarian. Not a vegan. A mild vegetarian.

ALEC "A mild vegetarian"? There's nae such thing! It's like sayin' somebody's had an uncomplicated heart attack!

SMILER Problem solved, Alec. You open the bottle of sherry you won in that raffle years ago. She'll have no idea whit she's eatin' after a coupla glasses o' that. Where's she stayin', by the way?

WILMA We'll book her into Mrs. McNab's B & B for the four days.

SMILER Fingers crossed George is away havin' his treatment. Although he might as well stick his heid in a microwave twice a day for all the benefit he seems to get from it.

WILMA I think George is a nice lad.

SMILER He might be nice, right enough, but he's daft as a brush.

ALEC Vegetarian! That's my plans for food for the week oot the windae.

WILMA Don't be silly, Alec. It's no big deal. I'll sort it out.

ALEC Five weeks ago my life was normal. Now it's like livin' in a minefield.

SMILER Alec, I hardly think you can compare livin' with a vegetarian for four days to pickin' your way through a field of unexploded bombs.

ALEC You shut yir face, you.

A woman appears. As she draws level –

SMILER [*nodding in greeting*] Jinty.

JINTY [*nodding in greeting*] Smiler.

She walks on and away.

WILMA Smiler.

SMILER Whit?

WILMA Don't ignore me, Smiler. I'm fascinated. Who is she? She certainly gets around, doesn't she? What's the story, Smiler?

SMILER I broke Jinty's heart when I dumped her. She swore she'd haunt me. An' she does.

WILMA I wouldn't know, but she looks like she might be a nice woman.

SMILER You know nothin', Wilma. She's an Ayr United supporter.

WILMA It's none of my business, but I think you ought to speak to her, not just nod and let her walk off. Life's too short.

SMILER You think so?

WILMA Up to you.

SMILER Alec, you should see your face. I wish I had a mirror. Brighten up, for heaven's sake. Listen, if we walk back that way, we can catch the bus on the other side of Drumley Woods.

ALEC The stop at the Toll is much nearer.

SMILER Aye, but if we go through Drumley Woods, we can fill our pockets wi' tree bark.

ALEC What would I be wantin' wi' tree bark?

SMILER Make a big pot o' tree bark soup for Wilma's lassie.

INT. FRONT ROOM OF B & B. AFTERNOON.
Betty and Isobel are sitting with cups of tea.

BETTY So, Canada. Is it a big place?

ISOBEL You could say that.

BETTY I did. I'll tell you where's a big place : Edinburgh. It just goes on and on. I went there with my husband Edward once, before he contracted senility. We went on a Mystery Coach trip. An' what a con that was.

ISOBEL [*polite*] A con?

BETTY You'd think they'd fence off a chunk of the country some-where to be used only for Mystery Coach tours, nothing else, wouldn't you? That we'd be driven somewhere and they'd open a gate and let the bus into this fenced-off, mystery part of Scotland. But no, he went straight up to Edinburgh. We'd have sued them, if we'd knew how. Edinburgh was lovely, but. And big, like I said.

Reaching and offering –

Are you quite sure you won't have a small dod of cake? It's exclu-sive to Spar's.

ISOBEL Quite sure, thank you. It's very kind of you. I ought to be moving. Check whether they're home yet.

BETTY Finish your tea up. There's no panic. It's not often I get the chance to sit and have a blether. An' you never know when there'll be an opportunity again. It's only the four days you're here for?

ISOBEL I fly back on Saturday.

BETTY As I said, I'm not back till Sunday, but you should manage fine. Just ask George if there's anything you need. Actually, it's definitely Fate that we can put you up. I'm a great believer in Fate. I read ma stars every morning without fail. You see, George – my son – normally would be away for a day or two, but his appointment got changed, and his is the only guest room. We're a small, family establishment, you see. But I'm away for five days, so my room's available. You'll meet George later. He's up on the hill at the moment, collecting sheep shite for the window-box. Are you regular yourself?

ISOBEL [*lost*] I'm sorry?

BETTY You know – Number Twos? There's quite a lot of women in this area suffer from bad constipation, and the funny thing is, it turns out most of them are bowlers. In the Patna Bowling Club. I hate bowling, but I've joined for the company and the conversation. It's right what they say : a problem shared is a problem halved. Anyway, we're off to Largs for the Scottish Championships. Would you be paying in advance?

ISOBEL I can do. Is Visa O.K?

BETTY Well, seeing as you're Alec Gourlay's niece, you don't have to leave your passport. And cash'll be great if you've got it. I'll just go and find my Receipt Book. I think it might be in the loft.

She goes, leaving Isobel fairly confused. The dog comes in and looks around. Isobel encourages it to come to her. She is about to unlace the muzzle when George appears, a brown paper bag in his hand. When he sees what she plans, he shakes his head vigorously.

ISOBEL Don't take the muzzle off?

He shakes his head. She leaves the muzzle on.

You must be George?

He nods.

I'm Isobel. Isobel Gourlay. I'm booked in for four days.

He just stands. Longish pause. To make conversation, she indicates the bag.

ISOBEL [*ct'd*] A successful afternoon?

He nods, and the wet bottom of the bag splits, and sheep shit cascades all over the carpet.

INT. THE PATNA BUS. LATE AFTERNOON.
Wilma and Smiler are sitting together. Alec is on his own. The bus has stopped to let a sheep cross the road.

BUS DRIVER If that animal disnae move, a venison supper's on the cards tonight, right enough.

ALEC You get venison fae deer, for heaven's sake!

BUS DRIVER Don't flaunt your education on ma bus, Alec Gourlay. Just thank your lucky stars I'm an understandin' sorta bloke. It's no' everybody would have let you away wi' forgettin' your bus pass.

ALEC Just cut the chat an' drive, will you? I widnae mind gettin' hame before Prince Charles gets crowned.

BUS DRIVER You've nothing tae get hame for, so don't go pretendin' otherwise.

The sheep has crossed. The bus continues its journey.

Ah, well, it looks like spaghetti hoops an' chips after all. As usual.

Alec sees something puzzling out of the window.

ALEC There's somebody at ma door.

All three peer out.

SMILER It'll be some mate o' Ida an' Bob Hyslop. One o' the God Squad to tell you you're headin' for hell fire if you don't change your ways.

ALEC It's no' me changin' ma ways. It's other people changin' them for me.

WILMA It's not someone from God. It's someone from Canada. That's your niece, Alec.

INT. LIVING ROOM. LATE AFTERNOON.

Alec, Smiler and Isobel sitting. The atmosphere is rather awkward.

SMILER So, how was the flight, Isobel?

ISOBEL Fine, thanks.

ALEC Did they give you a meal?

SMILER Alec, the lassie's just told us it took fourteen hours. They're bound to have given her a meal.

ALEC I was just wonderin' when she next needed to eat.

ISOBEL I'm fine, thanks.

ALEC Your mother'll make you a cup of tea as soon as she finishes in the lavatory. Is it normal tea you drink?

ISOBEL [*confused*] Sure.

SMILER So, you're already booked intae the B & B?

ISOBEL Yes, thanks. Barbara at the Swallow showed me where it was, and I thought I might as well fix it while I was waiting.

ALEC Did you tell Betty?

ISOBEL Sorry?

ALEC Did you tell Betty you were different?

She is very confused.

Vegetarian.

ISOBEL No, I will, though.

She tries to lighten things up.

It seemed like a nice place.

SMILER As long as you've seen "One Flew Over The Cuckoo's Nest", you'll have some idea what to expect.

She's confused again, but doing her best.

ISOBEL O, I forgot. Thank you for the presents you sent me, Uncle Alec.

Nobody's ever called him this before.

I should have said that straight away.

SMILER You liked them, then?

ISOBEL It was a lovely, lovely thought.

SMILER "The Broons" Annual, the thermal underwear and the Jimmy Shand cassette?

ISOBEL I was very touched.

SMILER Fair enough.

ALEC [*warming to her*] You're very welcome, hen. After all, you're the only niece I've got. Would you like to see some photographs?

ISOBEL I'd love to.

ALEC Smiler, get the shoe-box doon. [*to Isobel –*] I've got a little box full of photos and momentos.

Smiler moves a chair to stand on, feeling around the top of a wall cupboard.

SMILER If you kept this in a sensible place, Alec, it wouldn't need Spiderman to reach it.

ISOBEL Were you a coal miner as well, Mr. Fulton?

SMILER Smiler, hen. It's Smiler. Aye, I was. Like everybody else here. It was a toss-up between professional football, rocket scientry, brain surgery, or the pits. We all lost the toss.

He hands the box to Alec, who takes the lid off.

ALEC That's the school netball team, look. Jinty Muir the captain.

ISOBEL Lovely legs.

SMILER That was fifty years ago. Those thighs are ankles now. It's not the netball that's between her knees these days, it's her breasts. Excuse language, hen.

ALEC An' here's one of Smiler with his pigeons.

ISOBEL Pigeons?

SMILER I race pigeons.

ISOBEL That's fantastic!

SMILER I race them. I eat them. Not the racers, I don't eat them. But see a good pigeon, Isobel, marinated in red wine with some oven chips on the side – for you it would be like the Berlin Wall comin' down : the beginning of the end of vegetarianism. Do you know somethin', Alec? If you hadn't such abnormally big feet, this shoe-box would be a lot smaller, an' the past widnae have so much in it.

ISOBEL I've got a couple of things, Uncle Alec.

They watch as she looks in her handbag.

There's this.

She hands Alec a photograph. Smiler looks over Alec's shoulder.

SMILER In the name o' the wee man! Is that a woman, or the back end o' a bus?

ISOBEL It's my Gran. It's your Mom, Uncle Alec.

SMILER [*back-tracking*] Aye, well, I bet she was beautiful when she smiled.

EXT. GRAVEYARD. LATE AFTERNOON.

Alec and Smiler are strolling. A minibus marked "Patna Women's Bowling Club" drives out of the village.

SMILER There's the Constipation Coach off to Largs.

ALEC Is there any point at all tryin' tae understand women? They're a complete mystery. I'm just beginnin' tae get on fine wi' Isobel, an' her mother insists she has to go into Ayr again because there's somethin' she has to do. An' not tellin' us what. They're a complete mystery.

SMILER Your niece is a wee smasher, but.

ALEC Aye, you're right there. Nice lookin' girl as well. You know, over the years I've thought about ma mother maybe twice. In the last six weeks an awfy lot more, naturally. I don't want you tryin' tae make a joke about this, but I had it in ma mind, I don't know why, but I had it in ma mind she'd be a cross between Jane Russell and Lana Turner.

SMILER I think I've seen your mother before, Alec, if that photo's anythin' to go by. Pathe News in cinemas in the early 50's. Moscow. She was standin' next tae Stalin in the May Day parades.

ALEC Is there any point at all askin' you tae be serious, Smiler?

SMILER [*after considering*] Not a lot.

A woman appears on the path. Smiler nods in greeting.

Jinty.

JINTY [*nodding in greeting*] Smiler.

Jinty starts to walk away. Smiler indicates the graves.

SMILER [*to Jinty*] This is where all paths lead to right enough, eh?

Jinty faints.

EXT. PATNA BUS STOP. LATE AFTERNOON.
Wilma and Isobel are waiting. Wilma is carrying a copy of "The Ayrshire Post".

WILMA I could do this on my own, but it's an opportunity to hear your news. And we've not been on our own for a minute since you got here.

ISOBEL What is it you have to do, Mom?

WILMA I got a sudden urge to follow up something I noticed in the local newspaper. It might come to nothing. I'll explain later. What's more important is, how difficult are things back in Edmonton?

ISOBEL They're not easy. Everyone knows now, that although you put your name to it, it was me leaked the fraud story. They can't dismiss me, but they are able to make life at work pretty difficult. The atmosphere's horrible.

WILMA Can't you take a long vacation? I've got money. I could help you out.

ISOBEL I might be able to. I'll see what I can arrange when I go back. Maybe if I were able to go away for a month or so, the situation would begin to calm down. Maybe not.

The bowlers' minibus drives past. Betty waves. Isobel waves back.

Uncle Alec's nice, I think. Is he what you expected?

WILMA I had no idea what to expect, had I? I had no expectations. I sort of knew what I hoped he'd be like.

ISOBEL And is he what you'd hoped he'd be?

WILMA [*laughing*] No. Not at all. He's very different to what I'd imagined.

ISOBEL But that's good?

WILMA Yeah, that's good. I often think he's still four years old. And then his dentures click.

ISOBEL Why did you let the other bus go past? It said Ayr on the front.

WILMA It said, Ayr via Dalrymple.

ISOBEL What's wrong with Dalrymple?

WILMA Don't ask.

ISOBEL How long, do you think, before ours arrives?

WILMA Not long now. Unless the driver's stopped for venison.

ISOBEL Venison? Gosh! Are there deer in these parts?

WILMA [*matter of fact*] No.

INT. B & B FRONT ROOM. EVENING.
Isobel and George are sitting, Isobel drinking tea. The poodle's there.

ISOBEL This tea's lovely, thanks.

Silence.

Would you mind very much if I took the muzzle off the dog?

Silence, but then George nods. Carefully, she removes the muzzle. The dog's pretty happy. On the wall there's a photograph of a man fishing.

Is that your Dad?

George nods.

Is he a keen fisherman?

No response.

Might I meet him?

GEORGE Not here. He's not well.

ISOBEL O, I am sorry. I never knew my Dad. He left when I was very young. Too young to remember.

Silence.

We're all going over to the Swallow. Apparently there's a concert tonight. Will you be there?

George shakes his head.

It sounds like it might be fun.

INT. THE "SWALLOW" PUB. EVENING.
It's packed, and most of the customers are watching a football game on television. Alec, Wilma, Isobel and Smiler have a table. Jinty, a bandage round her head, is sitting in a corner. Barbara and Oswald are serving.

SMILER [*commentator's voice*] "And eighty million passes to fifty million, who is blocked by £170,000 a week!" Pit it aff! This has nothin' tae dae wi' twenty two blokes and a leather ball. It's twenty two bankers and a business logo on a shirt.

WILMA There'll be nae mair Shankleys noo!

SMILER You do catch on, hen. Maybe helped by four babychams, but you do catch on.

The Hyslop parents, formally dressed, come out.

Bob. Ida.

Nods all round.

Have a wonderful Prayer Meeting.

The Hyslops leave.

Some folk, wisely, will do anythin' to avoid one of Singer's Jim Reeves concerts.

SINGER makes a big entrance from up the back.

SINGER Silence! Can we have a wee bit o' silence, ladies an' gentlemen, please!

SMILER Somebody turn the television up!

SINGER Order! Order!

The general conversation subsides. Singer notices the game on the telly.

Whit's the score?

BARBARA Never you mind the score. Are you singin', or whit?

She turns the television off. A few groans.

It was a crap game, as you well know, so don't any of you be pretendin' you were enjoyin' it. Singer, the floor's yours.

SMILER Aye, an' the floor's more musical.

SINGER Well, anybody's welcome tae have a go if they think they're better.

SMILER You couldne even beat One-Lung Milby in the karaoke contest!

SINGER Well, let's hear you, then, Smiler. You're awfy handy wi' your mooth, but less handy puttin' your neck on the line.

All of this is good-natured. They all know Singer will begin in a moment or two.

WILMA [*suddenly*] Isobel can sing.

She's slightly louder than she meant to be, because of the alcohol. Everybody looks.

ISOBEL Mom, no!

WILMA I know you're shy, but I've heard you sing. You're a terrific singer. At least your Mom thinks so.

ISOBEL [*genuinely terrified*] Not in public, Mom, please! Not in front of strangers.

SINGER There's no strangers here, hen. Give us a wee tune. It'll be a nice warm-up for me. Let's all hear it for Alec Gourlay's wee niece all the way from Canada!

Whistles and applause.

A beautiful young songstress from across the water.

Alec squeezes her hand, and this tips the balance. A bit of her still dreading it, Isobel joins Singer.

You go ahead, hen. Whatever it is, I'll pick it up as we go along.

Isobel begins to sing "What A Difference A Day Made". Singer doesn't pick it up, of course, he just throws in a few random chords which he thinks might fit. More often than not, they don't, but Isobel grows increasingly confident. Oswald and Barbara lean together. Alec and Wilma hold hands proudly. Jinty catches Smiler's eye. Towards the end of the song, Isobel senses a movement at the window. Outside, looking in, unseen by the others, is George.

EXT. HILLSIDE. EVENING.

Wilma and Alec are climbing, Wilma leading with a torch.

ALEC [*puffing*] Is it the babychams has warped your brain? Did you stop off in Dalrymple on the way back from Ayr? Is there a full moon an' you're a witch? In the name o' the wee man, will you tell me why you've dragged me oot the pub an' miles across fields?

WILMA Not miles. Don't exaggerate. One mile, perhaps. Nearly there.

ALEC Nearly where?

WILMA Just be patient, Alec. Not far now.

They continue for a bit, then Wilma suddenly stops and examines the ground.

Do you know where we are?

ALEC [*after looking around*] Of course I know where we are. But I'm surprised you do. So, he told you.

WILMA Who told me?

ALEC Smiler.

WILMA Smiler? Smiler told me what?

ALEC This is the spot where he got Jinty Muir pregnant. The exact spot. I've stood here many's a day and pictured the brief event. But I must admit, I'm gobsmacked it's of any interest to you.

WILMA He told me no such thing.

ALEC He didnae?

WILMA No.

ALEC Then why are we here, but?

WILMA It's something you said this morning.

ALEC Whit did I say this morning? Look, I'm sorry I raised my voice at breakfast, but there really isn't anythin' worse than tea without sugar.

WILMA It wasn't the sugar.

ALEC Then whit was it?

WILMA What's the one thing you own that's too big to fit into a suitcase?

Alec thinks, then remembers.

ALEC The table in the living room.

WILMA Well, now you've got two things.

Alec is lost.

Your table and these three acres of land.

A long silence.

ALEC Whit??

WILMA I've arranged to buy this little piece of land.

ALEC For whit?

WILMA For a house.

ALEC is shocked and disbelieving.

ALEC In the name o' the wee man!

WILMA No. In the name of Wilma and Alec Gourlay.

And the moon comes out from behind a cloud.

Episode Four

INT/EXT. THE NEW HOUSE. MORNING.

Alec and Wilma are standing in the living room. There is no furniture and the room looks palatial.

ALEC No.

WILMA It'll cost you nothing to have a look around.

They move into the hall. Alec spots the bathroom. He goes in, flushes the toilet, and waits until it fills up again.

ALEC Magic.

WILMA It's not magic, it's plumbing.

ALEC I mean, magic that works. Mine doesn't.

WILMA Unless you "wallop it up an' doon" a few times. This house has two toilets, and I'm prepared to bet they both work.

ALEC The answer's still no.

WILMA And four bedrooms.

ALEC Whit use would we have for four bedrooms?

WILMA There's you. Me. Isobel, while she's here on vacation.

ALEC That still leaves one. I could put a big, elaborate model-railway in that one.

WILMA You certainly could.

ALEC If I happened tae be the slightest, tiniest bit interested in model-railways. So the answer's still no.

WILMA You said no to the plot of land, and I still don't understand why.

ALEC I said no, because I couldnae begin to contemplate living on the spot where Smiler and Jinty Muir writhed about on the grass with nae clothes on. Well, Jinty would have had nae clothes on. Smiler would have had his socks and bonnet.

WILMA That's a pathetic excuse.

ALEC Ma life's been disrupted enough in the last two months.

WILMA But look at the advantages. We're squashed in your old house.

ALEC Naebody asked you tae move in.

WILMA [*hurt*] O, Alec!

ALEC Sorry. Sorry, hen. I didn't mean that. Honest. No, it's been great meetin' ma twin sister after sixty years, an' all that, but it's taken a while tae cope wi' headin' for the lavatory of a mornin' an' realisin' there's somebody in there, an' realisin' it's no' me. But I have coped, an' it's fine, an' I've no regrets. But this is somethin' else.

WILMA But it could be a good something else.

ALEC It was the pit manager's hoose, for heaven's sake! That's why it's been lyin' empty for years. It's far an' away the biggest hoose in Patna! I'm just Alec Gourlay.

WILMA You're Alec Gourlay. Not "just Alec Gourlay".

ALEC I said no. I'm puttin' ma foot doon. I should put ma foot doon more often.

He walks out. Wilma follows. He's aware of conflict in the air, and unhappy about it. In front of him is a huge garden.

Look at that, for example. Who'd do the garden? I hate gardenin'. When you've spent thirty six years in the pits, you want tae give your back a rest.

WILMA We could employ someone. I've got the money.

ALEC No.

But this is a touch less insistent. They walk up the path, and as he closes the gate, Wilma turns him round to look back.

WILMA It's there, Alec. It's empty.

ALEC It's a funny thing, life, is it no'? See ma wee hoose wi' the dodgy toilet? Three months ago I'd have put every penny I had on leavin' that hoose in an ambulance or a coffin. An' only yesterday I'd have put every penny I had on *both* of us leavin' that hoose in an ambulance or a coffin.

WILMA And today?

Alec points to the drive-way.

ALEC I suppose the ambulance-man would have an easier job here. Nae problem for the hearse-driver either.

EXT. HILLSIDE. MORNING.

Isobel sits on the grass looking down on the village. George is collecting sheep shit. He finishes and joins her.

ISOBEL Which one is your house?

He points.

Got it. And where's Uncle Alec's?

He points again.

Know something? I've been here three weeks now and it feels much, much longer. But in a good way. I don't miss Canada at all. Have you lived here all your life, George?

He nods.

And you like it?

He shrugs. He wipes sheep shit off his hand and points.

Where? Where am I supposed to be looking? The big house? The big house just outside the village? With the red roof, is that the one you mean?

He nods.

Whose house is it?

No response.

That's the house you'd really like to live in?

He shakes his head vigorously.

Why don't you say?

But he doesn't.

The big house with the red roof. And you don't know who lives there.

He looks at her.

ISOBEL [*ct'd*] Or you do know who lives there?

He nods.

INT. LIVING ROOM. ALEC'S HOUSE. LATE MORNING.

Alec, Wilma and Smiler are having tea and scones.

SMILER Maybe I should start callin' you Lord Gourlay. I mean, you were conceived by a Mossblown lassie on a coach trip tae the Trossachs, an' a Peer of the Realm who was stuck for somethin' tae dae for two minutes, an' now here you are buying the biggest house in Patna.

ALEC It's no' me buyin' it. It's Wilma.

SMILER Aye, I know that, Alec. You can be awfy literal sometimes.

ALEC An' you can be awfy annoyin'.

SMILER I'm no' bein' annoyin'. Just commenting on reality. Boswell tae your Johnson.

ALEC Are you pished? It's only eleven o'clock.

SMILER I'm no' pished. These beautiful scones and tea that the lovely Wilma has just provided are my only elevenses, I promise you. You've got the wrong man there. It's Singer for whom elevenses is a coupla pints.

ALEC So what's brought this mood on?

SMILER I'm just enjoyin' watchin' you shift from bein' a retired miner whose highlight of the day was his morning hour in the toilet, tae somethin' like Prince Charles surrounded by estates an' women.

WILMA Alec, can I ask you a question?

ALEC You always worry me when you say things like that, but go ahead.

WILMA Perhaps I should ask you privately.

SMILER D'you want me oot for this?

WILMA No, no.

She leads a bewildered Alec into the hall and closes the door, leaving a puzzled Smiler.

SMILER [*calling*] If it's somethin' tae do wi' the toilet, I hivnae been in there since I arrived!

They come back in. Alec is smirking. They sit slowly and deliberately.

WILMA I wanted to ask you something, Smiler, but I had to check with Alec first.

SMILER So?

WILMA It's O.K. by Alec.

SMILER What's O.K. by Alec?

WILMA What I wanted to ask you.

SMILER So ask.

WILMA It's not a question, so much as an offer. We want to offer that you move into the new house with us.

It sinks in, and as Alec suspected, Smiler is terrified.

INT/EXT. ALEC'S HOUSE. MORNING.

The place is a shambles, with Smiler helping Alec to pack up. Alec lifts up a large cardboard box and takes it out. Smiler follows him with another. The garden is an Everest of stuff accumulated over decades, no matter how small the house. Everything from a mangle to a framed photo of Arthur Scargill. They heap the boxes on top of the pile. Alec sits on the step and undoes his laces.

ALEC I've got a stone in ma shoe.

SMILER The size o' they feet, it's a wonder you don't get bricks in them.

ALEC [*enjoying this*] It's been nearly a week, Smiler. An' we're still waitin'.

SMILER Don't rush me. It's too big a decision tae rush.

Stepping over Alec, he goes back into the house. He pulls open a cupboard overflowing with junk. Alec joins him. Smiler has found a bunch of decrepit artificial flowers.

ALEC You can dump them.

SMILER Hold your horses. You never know when they might come in handy.

ALEC They're a bunch o' plastic flowers covered in stoor!

But Smiler sets them aside anyway. They're sorting through things when Smiler comes across a box of diaries.

SMILER I never knew you kept diaries!

ALEC You don't know everythin' aboot me, Smiler.

SMILER I've known you since you were four. The only thing I don't know about you, is why you put a pound on Ayr United tae beat Hibs.

ALEC That was in 1961!

SMILER The year's no excuse, Alec. Anybody who puts a pound on Ayr United to beat anybody is either rat-arsed pished or been kidnapped in Dalrymple. [*reading*] "July 5th, 1988 – lashing with rain, so couldn't cut the grass. August 30th, 1991 – not a good idea to plant bulbs in these high winds. May 10th, 1994 – a family of birds playing in the garden. Weeding would only disturb them. December 14th, 1995 – I love it when it snows a lot. It makes every garden in Patna look the same ."

ALEC I hate gardenin'.

SMILER But yours is the size o' a pool table!

ALEC I still hate it.

SMILER The hoose that Wilma's bought – who's gonnae till the soil there if you don't?

ALEC You?

SMILER Don't push it, Alec!

By now they are in the garden again, adding to the mountain. Jinty arrives by the gate.

JINTY [*nodding in greeting*] Smiler.

SMILER [*nodding in greeting*] Jinty.

She starts to walk off.

Haw! Jinty!

She halts.

SMILER [*ct'd*] Hold on a minute, will you?

He goes into the house. A pause where no one is sure what to do. Eventually Alec indicates the rubbish.

ALEC Huge, eh?

JINTY Don't talk dirty in ma presence, Alec Gourlay!

Smiler appears with the flowers, dripping from where he's stuck them under a tap.

SMILER [*presenting them*] I thought you might like these.

She takes them. They look at each other. A moment that could be forty years old. She begins to move away.

JINTY [*calling back*] I'll put them in water right away. So's they'll keep for a while.

SMILER They don't need water, Jinty. They'll no' die. They're plastic. Permanent. They're no' bothered aboot water, Jinty!

But she's gone.

EXT. PATNA ROAD. AFTERNOON.
George and Isobel are walking towards the red-roofed house. George is wearing a tie. The red-roofed house is a Nursing Home.

INT. THE NURSING HOME. AFTERNOON.
George and Isobel are walking along a corridor. An elderly, white-haired man comes up to them. He seems perfectly normal, if slightly distressed.

ELDERLY MAN Do you know this area?

ISOBEL Not really.

ELDERLY MAN I cannae find what I'm lookin' for, you see. I've looked everywhere. But I can't find anywhere. I can't find anywhere for ma cows tae graze. Do you think if I go this way, I might find somewhere? If I go along here? Then I might find a place for ma cows tae graze?

ISOBEL [*uncomfortable*] Possibly. It's worth a try.

He rushes off in front of them. They continue walking, past a lounge area where half a dozen residents are either watching TV, moving around, talking to themselves, or all three. In worlds of their own. George and Isobel have reached a row of single rooms. Sitting on the edge of the bed in one of them is the white-haired man. George stops by the door.

ISOBEL Did you find a place for your cows to graze?

ELDERLY MAN Naw. I havnae found anywhere for ma cows tae graze.

ISOBEL O, dear.

ELDERLY MAN An' there's somethin' else.

ISOBEL And what's that?

ELDERLY MAN I havenae even found ma cows.

George steps towards the bed, looks at the man, looks back at Isobel.

GEORGE Ma Daddy.

INT/EXT. ALEC'S HOUSE. AFTERNOON.

Wilma and Smiler are standing in the bare living room.

SMILER Have you ever noticed whit a big head George McNab's got. Disproportionate to the rest of his body?

WILMA I can't say I have.

SMILER Well, if he hisnae, he should have. I'm just standin' here thinkin' how everythin' looks bigger empty.

WILMA The garden looks like a bomb's been dropped.

SMILER It always did. It was always a disgrace. In the coupla months you've been here, don't tell me you've never noticed.

WILMA There's so little of it.

SMILER True enough. An' the day before we met you, the day before you arrived, Alec bribed Singer to tidy it up.

WILMA Bribed him?

SMILER With a Jim Reeves CD he got in Oxfam in Ayr. Singer was over the moon. All he needs now is a CD player.

WILMA I've realised Alec doesn't enjoy gardening.

SMILER Alec has the same sort o' relationship to gardenin' as Ayr United does to scorin' goals : the two are incompatible.

He checks his watch.

Where's Singer got to wi' the lorry?

WILMA Stuck behind a flock of sheep, perhaps?

SMILER Stuck behind a few pints o' heavy, mair like.

They have walked into the garden.

Do you really like Patna, Wilma?

WILMA I love Patna.

SMILER That's a sentence I never thought I'd hear uttered.

WILMA Don't you love it, Smiler?

SMILER I never think aboot it. I've lived here all ma life. Patna's Patna. It's just there.

WILMA You've never thought of leaving?

SMILER Naw. Not even when I was workin' an' the pits were open, an' I had some money. I sometimes used to think aboot the Wild West. Like day-dream. Cattle-ranching an' guns. But there are nae pits in the Wild West, are there? Listen, look. See what turned up in the loft? I was on my own, about half an hour ago, clearin' the last o' the loft oot, an look! Alec got this for Christmas when he was about eight. He was always rubbish at it, but I was great.

He has pulled a holster and two toy guns out of a packing case. He tucks one gun into his belt, and places the other one on the ground in front of Wilma. He does his cowboy voice.

Pick up the gun.

WIlma hesitates. Smiler goes back to normal.

You're the baddie, O.K? You're not a woman, you're the baddie.

He goes cowboy again.

Pick up the gun.

She grabs for it. He draws and "shoots" her.

Nae chance. I'm too fast, you see.

WILMA Smiler?

SMILER Whit?

WILMA Why don't you come and live with us? There's an extra room. No rent. The three of us. You've had a week to think about it now. Alec bets you won't. He jokes about it. He says, how can we have a man in the house who'll happily pare the corns off his feet with a razor blade before eating a fish supper, and never a hand-wash in the gap? But he'd like that. And so would I.

SMILER I was faster than anybody in Patna. An' some o' them were fast. But I was always faster. Everybody knew it. I was a kind o' legend wi' the gun. It's a funny thing, life, is it no'?

WILMA What do you say?

SMILER I say, if there were real bullets in this, I'd put the wind up Singer when he gets here. Always the same. He says three o'clock an' you're lucky if you see him on the same day. Bampot. He might think he sings like Jim Reeves or Frank Sinatra, but he drives like Stevie Wonder.

INT. THE "SWALLOW" PUB. EVENING.

Barbara and Oswald are serving. Barbara's parents are on their way upstairs. Isobel is by the bar.

BARBARA You mean like a kind of house-warming?

ISOBEL Yeah. Tomorrow night. You'd be more than welcome, Mr. and Mrs. Hyslop.

IDA No thank you, dear. The Prayer Meeting's here tomorrow. Upstairs.

The Hyslops go up.

BARBARA How many people would you say, roughly?

ISOBEL I think Uncle Alec plans to come in here later on and invite everybody.

BARBARA Everybody! In the name o' the wee man! I mean, I can do you the booze at discount right enough, but it's still gonna cost a fortune. They'll all be bringin' their intravenous drips.

ISOBEL My mom's paying. She's not bothered about the cost. She wants to do it.

BARBARA Fair enough. So shall I just get a load o' stuff, as much as I think, an' bring it across in the mornin', or somethin'?

ISOBEL That'd be great.

OSWALD What's the new house like?

ISOBEL Uncle Alec can't get over the amount of space.

BARBARA Naw. When you've been livin' in a shoe-box, I suppose that house would seem like Buckingham Palace. Mind you, considerin' the size of your Uncle Alec's feet, his old house likely wisnae as big as his shoe-box.

Singer, slightly dazed, appears at the bar.

SINGER Pint o' heavy, Oswald. And rapid, if you don't mind. I think I fell asleep in the toilet. Whit time is it?

ISOBEL Twenty after seven.

BARBARA He's not interested in that kind of accuracy, Isobel. [*to Singer*] It's Wednesday.

SINGER Wednesday?

BARBARA The one between Tuesday an' Thursday.

SINGER Wednesday? Is that no' the day Alec Gourlay was movin'?

ISOBEL He's moved.

SINGER Did I help him? Was I there at three o'clock wi' the van to shift some stuff?

Isobel shakes her head.

It's a funny life, is it no'? So, tomorrow's Thursday, is it?

He raises his glass.

Here's tae Thursday, eh?

INT. THE NEW HOUSE. EVENING.

The living room has been transformed, insofar as you can't move for beer cans and take-away cartons. In one area –

JINTY [*wiping her mouth*]   That was smashin'! There's nobody does Balti like Abdul. A sliver of chewin' tobacco will just dae the trick noo.

She brings out a coil of black tobacco and begins to cut it. She turns to her neighbour.

It's a while since you brought me a letter.

POSTMAN   It's a while since I brought anybody a letter. This is Patna. Are you no' gonnae eat the rest o' they chips?

She shakes her head mid-chew.

No point in them goin' tae waste, is there? Not when there are people starvin' in Dalrymple.

Elsewhere –

ALEC   Know somethin', Smiler? In the mornin', when there's just me an' Wilma an' Isobel here, it's like "The Loneliness Of The Long Distance Runner" in this room. If I go oot for the sugar, ma porridge is cold by the time I get back tae ma chair. It's like a bloody castle, this hoose.

But Smiler isn't playing.

WILMA   Full circle.

ALEC   Whit?

WILMA   That we end up in what seems like a castle to you. Our father probably owned a real castle.

ALEC   If he had this long to walk tae get the sugar, I'm surprised he had the energy to impregnate a wee lassie he met in the woods. His woods.

Both Wilma and Alec are merry, pleasantly sozzled.

WILMA   I suspect it wasn't all one-sided. She wasn't the soul of virtue – our mother.

ALEC   Well, I widnae know about that, me bein' abandoned at the age of four.

WILMA   Don't be bitter, Alec. That's all in the past. I think we could be heading for a happy ending, don't you?

ALEC Aye, you're right. I'm not bitter. I just hope the guide-dog had a good life.

This one is for Smiler's benefit.

WILMA What guide-dog?

ALEC Our father's guide-dog. Smiler hit the nail on the head, you know. The photo that Isobel brought over for me. I mean, not to put too fine a point on it, our mother looked like she'd been run over by a lorry. At least twice.

Smiler's not biting.

WILMA Maybe it was guilt, but I somehow think she made a great effort to appear unattractive.

ALEC Well, she succeeded right enough. You, however, you must get your looks from your father.

WILMA Thank you, kind sir.

ALEC Plus, you make a crackin' plate o' porridge.

He's noticed something.

Even George McNab is here.

WILMA With Isobel.

ALEC *Sittin'* with Isobel. Not *with* her. Sittin' with her.

Elsewhere –

Oswald, Barbara, Isobel and George are a group. Barbara is snogging Oswald.

OSWALD You're making me blush.

BARBARA Well, there's only you can tell. Did you know Oswald's studyin' medicine? Gynaecology, to be precise. But we don't say that in the pub. We say "doctor" in the pub.

ISOBEL What's your subject at University, Barbara?

BARBARA Mathematics. It runs in the family. Before ma father bought the Swallow, he was the bookie here.

ISOBEL Bookie?

BARBARA Bookmaker. Ran the betting-shop. I grew up with trebles and double-cross-mixes. The advanced physics of redundant coal miners spreading a £3 bet across eight races. They'd have left Einstein behind, I'm tellin' you.

Elsewhere –

WILMA Are you absolutely sure you don't want anything to eat, Smiler?

SMILER No thanks, Wilma. I've got a wee treat for later in the oven at hame.

Abdul joins them.

ABDUL Everythin' alright, Mr. Gourlay?

ALEC Fine, Abdul. Just great. Listen, Abdul, I wanted to ask you somethin'. Know ma old hoose?

ABDUL Aye.

ALEC Well, when I ordered a take-away, how long, roughly, would you say it took to get it from your shop to me in your wee motorbike?

ABDUL I don't know, Mr. Gourlay. Aboot four minutes, maybe.

ALEC Four minutes?

ABDUL Somethin' like that.

ALEC Four minutes. Fair enough. Now, the next question is this : how long, would you say, from your shop to this new house on the bike?

ABDUL To here? A coupla minutes.

ALEC Two minutes. Exactly half the time. We seem tae be agreed on that. So, the subject I wanted tae broach, Abdul, was discounts on your delivery charges.

Elsewhere –

Barbara is passing Betty.

BARBARA You cannae move in the kitchen through there for people eatin' vindaloo like there was no tomorrow.

BETTY That'll be the Ladies Bowling Club right enough. Just as well there are two toilets. It's a big hoose, is it no'?

BARBARA Very nice.

BETTY Have you been upstairs yet?

BARBARA Naw.

BETTY Quite nice. All new furniture, by the looks of it. Alec's twin sister must have had a few bob tae fork out. An' thank God she hasn't got her brother's taste. But I'll tell you somethin'. There's a framed photo at the top o' the stairs that's completely out of place, if you ask me.

BARBARA O, aye. Whit's that?

BETTY It's an' old woman. Well, at least I think it's a woman. It could be one o' they things you see on the Natural History programmes on the telly. One o' they creatures that never evolved.

Elsewhere –

The doorbell rings.

ALEC Who'd be phonin' us?

WILMA It's not the phone, it's the doorbell, Alec.

ALEC Is it? I never had either before.

SMILER It's the doorbell. It's Singer. He's tryin' tae play a tune on it. Unrecognisable, of course.

ALEC Listen, Smiler, is it a yes or a no? You must have decided by now.

SMILER I'll let you know tomorrow. Tomorrow.

ALEC Is that a promise?

SMILER Aye.

Elsewhere –

Oswald has a guitar. Singer produces his mouth-organ.

SINGER I'll kick off with a few well-loved song selections, if you don't mind.

OSWALD Not the usual stuff, mate, please. Something different. Please?

SINGER "She". Do you know "She"?

OSWALD "She"?

SINGER Aye, "She".

OSWALD I think I might be able to busk it. I'll do my best.

He tunes the guitar. Singer stands up. Oswald plays the intro and starts in on Charles Aznavour's "She".

SINGER "She gets too hungry for dinner at eight, She likes the theatre, but always comes late, She doesn't bother ... "

INT. SMILER'S LIVING ROOM. NIGHT.

Smiler is in his pyjamas. He sits at the table and reads what he's just written by pencil on lined notepaper.

SINGER "Dear Alec and Wilma, I have considered your kind offer long and hard and weighed it up, but even though youse have plenty of room and two toilets and all that, I have decided to stay where I am. It is easier to write than say, then we don't have to bring it up again. But thank youse both. Your pal, Smiler."

He adds one more sentence in barely joined-up writing.

"P.S. Also, I won't have to think twice when I get troubled with the wind."

On his way to find an envelope, he picks up the two guns and lays one on the floor in front of him.

Pick up the gun. Pick up the gun!

He draws, and shoots his invisible foe. He puts the guns away. There's a photo of his parents by the drawer.

You'll never guess where I've been tonight. You widnae believe the changes goin' on in Patna. Not me, though. You widnae notice much difference in your son. I don't know whether that's a good thing or not.

He puts the letter in an envelope and seals it. He goes to the cooker and opens the oven door. He pulls out the tray to reveal a marinating pigeon.

Serves you right for losin' the last three races, ya lazy bastard, ye. Be in ma stomach in aboot ten minutes, so you will. Just enough time for me tae have a go at ma corns.

And he sits, and takes his socks off, and he reaches for a razor blade.

Episode Five

INT. THE NEW HOUSE. MORNING.

Alec is on the toilet, his pyjama trousers round his ankles. He is drinking tea.

ALEC "Happy birthday tae me, happy birthday tae me, Happy birthday, dear Alec, happy birthday tae me."

INT. THE NEW HOUSE. MORNING.

Alec, still in his pyjamas, is at the kitchen table eating toast. The doorbell rings. He goes into the hall and considers picking up the telephone, but decides that it was, in fact, the doorbell. He opens the door to the postman.

ALEC How's it goin', Tam?

POSTMAN It's no' goin' very well, Alec, if you really want tae know.

ALEC How's that, Tam?

POSTMAN I'll tell you how's that, Alec. Thursday's normally a quiet day. I always bank on Thursday bein' a quiet day. On an average Thursday, in fact on every Thursday for about ten years now, even when it's Christmas, there's never anythin' to deliver in Patna. I just look intae the Post Office tae check, then I go back tae ma bed until about mid-day to catch up on the sleep I lose, seein' as I live next door tae an insomniac Bagpipe Major. But this mornin', when I go in, there's this parcel for your twin sister. Postmarked Canada.

Alec takes it.

ALEC Have you got nothin' for me?

POSTMAN Naw.

ALEC It's ma birthday.

POSTMAN It must be aboot fourteen million folk's birthdays. They cannae all get presents. The postal system would seize up.

He walks away. Alec goes back into the house to his toast. Smiler appears at the kitchen door.

SMILER I didnae want tae ring the doorbell an' confuse you.

ALEC I'm just up.

SMILER Are the lassies no' aboot?

ALEC Nae idea. It's ma birthday, Smiler.

SMILER O, aye, so it is. Happy birthday. Here you are.

He takes a book from his pocket.

ALEC Thanks a bunch, Smiler. You're a pal. You're a big saftie, really, aren't you?

He reads.

"Racing Pigeons – A Practical Guide To The Sport".

He slams the book shut.

Racing pigeons! You might as well have brought a book in Swahili about polar bears! I am not the slightest, tiniest bit remotely interested in pigeons!

SMILER [*innocent*] Is that right?

ALEC How long have you known me?

SMILER Sixty years.

ALEC An' have I ever, even once, in all that time, even for a nanosecond, shown the faintest curiosity about pigeons?

SMILER Naw, right enough. I was maybe a wee bit thoughtless there.

ALEC You'll not have read it, I suppose?

SMILER Naw, it looks good, but. Maybe I could read it after you. There's an idea, eh? Whit else did you get?

ALEC Nothin' yet.

SMILER So what's this?

There's a box with a ribbon on a side-table.

ALEC That's fae Isobel.

SMILER Whit is it?

ALEC Nae idea.

SMILER Are you gonnae open it?

ALEC Best wait tae Isobel's here.

SMILER Seems a shame to just let it sit there. She'll no' mind. She's Canadian. Chances are it's somethin' you'll hate anyway. You were never lucky wi' presents. Open it when she's not here to see your inevitable disappointment. Then you can lie when she gets back. Tell her you liked it. I'm nothin', Alec, if I'm not thoughtful.

INT. PATNA BUS. LATE MORNING.
Alec and Smiler are the only passengers. Alec is wielding a video-camera.

ALEC [*to the Bus Driver*] See this? For the cost o' this I could travel from Patna tae Ayr thousands o' times, it's that expensive.

BUS DRIVER You've got a bus pass. You travel free.

ALEC It's ma birthday. I got this from ma wee niece. Is it no' great?

BUS DRIVER See that sign there? It says you're no' supposed tae talk tae me when I'm drivin'. It's illegal. I could make a citizen's arrest, if I had a mind tae.

The drive continues. Alec is experimenting with the camera.

I've got a philosophy about birthdays. Shall I tell you my philosophy? They all end in tears. There's always somethin' goes wrong. So don't get your hopes up. No birthday present bears comparison tae a big plate o' chips.

EXT. ANNBANK WOODS. AFTERNOON.
Alec and Smiler are walking.

ALEC I wonder if I should have waited till she was there. I hope she'll no' be upset.

SMILER Life's too short, Alec. You have tae live every second to the full. See that wee insect doon there? Well, I could have stepped on it, and wallop! Dead. An' all the while it was thinkin' it had a lifetime ahead of it. See whit I'm tryin' tae say? I mean, for all we know, in the Insect Kingdom it could be that wee insect's birthday, an' out of politeness it's no' gonnae open its presents till the rest o' the insect family get back. An' what happens? I crush it with ma shoe, an' it never gets the use o' the presents, even briefly. Get ma drift?

ALEC Smiler.

SMILER Whit?

ALEC You just stepped on it.

SMILER Did I? I didnae mean to. Chances are it was on its last legs anyway. Riddled wi' malaria. I probably did it a favour, puttin' it oot its misery. Everythin' in this world has a reason, Alec. Except goin' tae watch Ayr United.

ALEC [*pointing*] There was a pit there.

SMILER Annbank Number Nine. Up at the top of the brae here was the Kingsway Cinema. I want you tae film me on that spot. Where we went whenever we came to Annbank to visit ma Auntie Jean. The Kingsway Cinema.

ALEC Don't romanticise it. It was a corrugated iron hut.

SMILER It might have been a corrugated iron hut, but it showed three different films a week. Six, if you include the B films. An' mainly cowboy.

ALEC It was a flea-pit! The most expensive seats were ninepence! There was no toilet. No heatin'. In winter people fought to get a wall seat because you could warm your hands on the corrugated iron that men were standin' outside pishin' against.

SMILER It was still the cradle o' ma dreams, even if you did catch some notifiable disease every time you went.

They are walking.

ALEC This is a great birthday, so it is. Not a cloud of any sort on the horizon, life-wise nor weather-wise, eh?

They reach the edge of the wood.

It was aboot here, wasn't it?

SMILER It was exactly here. It's carved in ma memory. One o' those things you can never lose or get rid of.

A woman appears from the direction of the village.

JINTY [*nodding in greeting*] Smiler.

SMILER [*nodding in greeting*] Jinty.

She is about to walk away.

Jinty, did you know this is where the Kingsway Cinema was? Did you ever go there?

JINTY Just the once. I caught chicken-pox.

SMILER Whit film was it?

JINTY I forget. I scratched all the way through it.

ALEC The place was a legend. For years whenever anybody anywhere in Ayrshire went tae the doctor's, the first question he'd ask would be, "Have you been tae the Kingsway Cinema in Annbank recently?"

SMILER Stop exaggeratin' an' get the camera oot.

Alec brings the video camera out of his plastic carrier-bag.

JINTY That's really somethin'.

ALEC [*chuffed*] I know. Ma niece – ma twin sister's wee lassie – gave it tae me for ma birthday.

JINTY No, I mean the carrier-bag. Is it one o' them Bags For Life? The ones they'll replace for ever an' ever?

SMILER I wish I'd brought the guns. You could have filmed me on the draw. I could use a bit o' wood.

ALEC Please yoursel'.

Smiler tucks a bit of a branch into his belt.

SMILER Are you filming?

ALEC Aye.

Smiler confronts Jinty.

SMILER [*cowboy*] Pick up the gun.

JINTY Whit gun?

SMILER [*cowboy*] The gun.

JINTY There's nae gun.

ALEC Do you want to try that again?

SMILER Naw. I need ma gun. We'll have tae come back another day.

JINTY So, is that a camera?

SMILER Naw, it's a cooker.

ALEC It certainly is a camera. One of the best birthday presents I've ever had in ma life. I must find out when Isobel's is. And Wilma's.

He is putting the camera away. Smiler is adjusting his belt. They look at each other, and, at exactly the same moment, the penny drops.

INT. THE NURSING HOME. LATE AFTERNOON.
Eddie – George's Dad – is in his room in his armchair. George and Isobel are perched on the bed. Nobody speaks. George takes his Dad's hand. The old man looks at both of them. He takes his hand away, but not significantly. Then Isobel says it.

ISOBEL We've got some news, Mr. McNab.

INT. SHOP IN AYR. LATE AFTERNOON.
ALEC I'm sorry I had tae borrow money. It never crossed ma mind that I'd need extra. I don't know why I bother carryin' ma card around, because I can never remember ma pin number.

SMILER Mine's easy. 1964. The last year Ayr United had a team that didnae play like eleven gigglin' big lassies.

ALEC I've just nae idea whit tae get her.

SMILER Get her the same as I've just bought her. Denture Soak an' Air Freshener. Cannae go wrong there.

ALEC She's ma sister, but. I have tae get her somethin' unusual, somethin' special. They slippers look quite nice.

SALES ASSISTANT Can I help youse?

ALEC Eh, just havin' a look at your slippers.

SALES ASSISTANT Whit size?

ALEC To be honest, I don't know.

SALES ASSISTANT [*asessing his feet*] At least a twelve, I'd say.

ALEC O, they're no' for me. They're for ma twin sister.

SALES ASSISTANT Well, if she's an identical twin, I'd say a twelve.

ALEC She's no' identical. She's a woman.

SALES ASSISTANT I've got the same size feet as ma man.

ALEC Is that right?

Her mobile phone rings.

SALES ASSISTANT [*to Alec*] Excuse me one moment, sir. [*into phone*] Aye, it's me ... No, I've got the tatties. You just buy a tin ... Aye, we'll have spaghetti hoops an' chips. Your favourite ... Aye, well, I'll see you later ... Cheerio. [*to Alec and Smiler*] That was ma man. He's a bus driver. It's our wedding anniversary today. I'm cookin' tonight. Spaghetti hoops an' chips. His favourite. He would eat shite if there was chips on the plate.

She offers her mobile phone.

Do you want tae ring your sister an' get the size o' her feet?

ALEC Naw, it's got tae be a surprise, you see. We'll just have a wee wander an' see what else there is. Happy Anniversary, by the way.

SALES ASSISTANT Thanks very much.

They wander off, eyes peeled for a possible gift.

YOUNG CHILD I want they trainers!

MOTHER Well, you're no' gettin' they trainers!

YOUNG CHILD But I want them! They can light up!

MOTHER I don't care if they can talk, you're no' gettin' them! Look at the price o' them! Do you think I'm made o' money?

YOUNG CHILD I'll start screamin' if I don't get them!

MOTHER You start screamin' an' you'll get nae sweeties for a week!

YOUNG CHILD Don't care!

MOTHER You start screamin' an' I'll tell your father when we get hame!

YOUNG CHILD Still don't care!

MOTHER You start screamin' an' I'll throw you aff the bus at Dalrymple!

YOUNG CHILD I've just thought, Mammy. They trainers are manky. Horrible. The shoes I've got on will do me for years. Honest, they will, Mammy.

SMILER [*elsewhere now*] Whit aboot a bra, Alec?

ALEC Don't be daft! I cannae buy her a bra! It's too personal.

SMILER She's your sister, for heaven's sake!

LINGERIE ASSISTANT Can I help youse, sir?

SMILER I was just lookin' at that bra.

LINGERIE ASSISTANT Very popular, this one, sir. And the size?

Smiler looks to Alec.

ALEC [*shrugging*] Nae idea.

SMILER She's about Jinty's size, would you say?

ALEC Maybe a wee bit bigger.

Smiler thinks for a moment, then holds his arm out, his hand cupped as though grasping a large grapefruit.

SMILER This size, hen.

INT. THE NEW HOUSE. LATE AFTERNOON.

Alec and Smiler come into the living room, where Wilma is.

ALEC Happy birthday, Wilma!

WILMA Happy birthday, Alec!

A big hug.

I was wondering where you'd got to.

ALEC We were tryin' the camera out. Do you think Isobel'll be upset I opened it when she wisnae here?

WILMA Of course she won't. Do you like it?

ALEC   It's fantastic. Absolutely unbelievable. We went tae Annbank an' tried it oot. Best birthday present I ever got in ma life. An' here's yours, Wilma. Bit awkward tae wrap, so I didnae bother. I know you'll no' mind.

She takes garden shears out of a bag.

SMILER Happy birthday, Wilma.

He hands over the denture soak and air freshener.

WILMA [*to Alec*] I knew you hadn't forgotten.

ALEC Forgotten? Whit are you talkin' aboot?

WILMA I know it sounds stupid, but you never once mentioned that it'd be my birthday as well, and I thought that maybe it hadn't crossed your mind that ...

ALEC We'd have had to be very stupid, extremely stupid, not to realise that ma twin sister's birthday is on the same day as mine. I mean, this is Alec Gourlay an' Smiler Fulton you're dealin' with, not George McNab.

WILMA I don't think George is stupid. He's different, that's all.

ALEC You're entitled tae your opinion, of course, even if it is ridiculous.

He is prowling.

As I say, Isobel's present was just amazin'.

WILMA And now you're wondering where mine is.

ALEC [*lying*] Not at all.

Wilma goes out.

SMILER Wonder what it'll be, Alec?

ALEC I'm awfy excited, Smiler.

SMILER So you should be. The last thing she bought you was a hoose.

Wilma returns with a bulky gift. Alec rips the paper off. It's a thick, brightly-coloured sweater. Smiler jumps back.

SMILER [*ct'd*] It's, eh, a wee bit loud, but very nice.

WILMA Let's see it on you, Alec.

ALEC I'd be too warm in it.

WILMA O, go on.

ALEC Tomorrow, maybe.

WILMA Don't you like it?

ALEC I like it fine. It's great. You really want tae see it on?

WILMA Yeah.

ALEC Fair enough.

He goes out.

WILMA So, you got the camera working, Smiler?

SMILER We're movie-makers now, Alec an' me. We filmed out the bus window. We filmed where the old picture house was in Annbank. Movie-makers, us.

WILMA So you're an expert with the red button now?

SMILER Whit red button's that, then?

INT. THE "SWALLOW" PUB. EVENING.
Alec and Smiler are at a table with Singer. Barbara and Oswald are behind the bar. Barbara is wearing dark glasses.

BARBARA [*calling out*] Sunglasses! Get your sunglasses here! Protect your retinas! Free pairs of sunglasses behind the bar!

ALEC Very funny, I don't think.

SINGER I'm never lucky wi' presents either, Alec. Mind you gave me that Jim Reeves CD for doin' your garden? Great present, but I've got nothin' tae play it on. An' one year at Christmas, somebody gave me a ticket for a Frank Sinatra concert in Glasgow. I couldnae sleep for weeks. I went all the way up tae Glasgow, an' it wisnae him. It was Frank somebody else. Didnae even have blue eyes. Sang all these arias from Wagner an' Handel an' Mozart an' Bizet. Wisnae even in English. Couldnae fathom a word o' it. Nae melody. Couldnae even hum along. An' they didnae even sell crisps or anythin'. An' it was a Sunday, so I missed "Sing Something Simple" on the wireless. So I know how you feel, Alec, right enough.

ALEC I did fine. I got a state-o'-the-art video camera from ma niece. Smiler an' me's been oot filmin' all afternoon. We got some great footage.

SMILER You might be jumpin' the gun there, Alec. We should maybe have lingered over the instruction book a wee bit longer, before racin' oot an' thinkin' we were David Lean.

ALEC Whit's that supposed tae mean?

SMILER I don't think we actually made use of the button that takes the camera off stand-by.

ALEC In the name o' the wee man!

SMILER You win some, you lose some. That bus driver wisnae far wrong. But never mind. Alec's sister's bakin' a cake, an' we're goin' back tae watch a home-video she got sent on from Canada.

Barbara's mother is on her way out, clutching a bible.

Ida.

IDA Smiler. Alec. Singer.

SMILER Must be a blessin', Ida, when Barbara is on holiday from the University. Means you can get a lot more Prayer Meetings in, eh?

She nods and goes.

I know I shouldn't be sayin' this in the presence of her daughter, so forgive me in advance, Barbara, but that woman's got some arse on her.

Betty comes in.

BARBARA Mrs. McNab! In the Swallow! A sight I thought I'd never see! What's the occasion?

BETTY Do you sell brandy?

BARBARA Aye. D'you want one?

BETTY I want a half bottle. To take away. No, make that a bottle.

SMILER Have you had the bill for George's treatment, Betty? The electricity bill?

BETTY You'll be laughin' on the other side o' your face before long.

Barbara fetches a bottle. Betty pays.

An' you an' all, Alec Gourlay. You, especially.

She goes. There's a puzzled pause.

SMILER Maybe somebody told her brandy was a laxative.

INT. THE NEW HOUSE KITCHEN. EVENING.

Wilma is icing a cake.

WILMA You're sure?

ISOBEL I'm sure.

WILMA I don't know what to say.

ISOBEL Then don't say anything. Just give me a hug.

They have a long hug.

I wasn't looking for it, believe me, Mom. It just happened.

WILMA Rather suddenly. But then, when it does, I suppose it does. Suddenly. Who else knows?

ISOBEL We told his mother about an hour ago.

WILMA And how did she take it?

ISOBEL I think she was stunned. She barely responded. I left them on their own for a bit. It'll take time to sink in. What are you thinking, Mom?

WILMA I'm thinking you're brave. I'm thinking the world's a different place than it was when I was your age. And yet I'd started thinking it wasn't such a different place, having come into this ... time-warp called Patna.

ISOBEL I know what you mean.

WILMA I wish I did.

ISOBEL Patna was ... Cupid.

WILMA I bet nobody's ever called it that before now. The practicalities are enormous, of course.

ISOBEL I know. I need you on my side, Mom.

WILMA I have absolutely no idea how Uncle Alec's going to take this. He's my brother and I love him to bits, even though I've only really known him for a matter of months, but I have absolutely no idea how he's going to react. In some ways he's the most predictable man I've ever met. Show him a lawnmower and he'll run a mile. Put salt on his chips before the vinegar, and he'll sulk for hours. But this ... ?

ISOBEL I'm scared.

WILMA I know you're scared. That's why I said you're brave. You need to be scared to be brave. I'm scared. I don't want any ... cracks, know what I mean? I'm as happy here as I've ever been in my life, and I didn't expect to be, and I'd rather there weren't any ... dislocations. I'd hate those. I'm not sure I'm strong enough to cope with those. But wobbles I can take. I can survive wobbles. So, cross fingers for a wobble, eh?

INT. THE NEW HOUSE. EVENING.
Alec and Smiler have beers. Wilma has a sherry. There's a birthday cake on the table.

ALEC It's a long time since I remember such a perfect day.

SMILER It'd be when they told you that you didn't need that second course of enemas.

ALEC Should we make a start on the cake, or should we wait until Isobel gets back, wherever she is? I haven't set eyes on her all day. She'll have expected me tae open her present by now, will she no'?

WILMA She will. No problem there. But maybe we should delay the cake.

ALEC Whatever you say, darlin'. Shall we start the video, but? She'll have already seen it.

WILMA Sure.

Wilma puts the home video on. There's film of Isobel throwing stones into a lake, disturbing the still water. Then Isobel opening Christmas presents in a kind of solitary way. She's shy, doesn't enjoy the limelight of the camera. Then Grandma and Wilma walking towards the camera until Grandma is in extreme close-up. Smiler pushes the pause button.

SMILER Lon Chaney. That's who she reminds me of. I knew it was somebody.

ALEC A wee bit o' respect, Smiler. That's our mother.

SMILER Here was us thinkin' she came from Mossblown, but I'm beginnin' tae think all the evidence points tae Dalrymple.

ALEC Lon Chaney I can take, Smiler. Boris Karloff I could take. But Dalrymple's out of order.

SMILER Maybe the picture's distorted wi' all that brightness comin' off your jumper.

ALEC It's funny, seein' ma mother on film, I tell you. She gave birth tae me, four years later she vanishes, denying her reponsibilities, an' now here she is, in the front room wi' us. An' two years dead.

SMILER Are you sure she's no' dead on the film there?

ALEC Smiler, you're out of order again!

WILMA I don't mind, really.

SMILER See? Wilma's a realist. What's the point o' tellin' lies? The woman's got a face like a camel's arse. What are friends for, if not to be honest?

Isobel appears in the doorway. Alec jumps up.

ALEC Ah, ma wee niece! Ma wee darlin'! Where have you been? Listen, was it O.K. I opened the present? The camera?

ISOBEL Of course. Happy birthday, Uncle Alec.

He gives her the most enormous hug. Over her shoulder he sees George standing there.

ALEC George! George, you really should ring the doorbell an' no' just walk intae folk's hooses, but seein' as it's you, an' seein' as it's ma birthday, I'll let it go this time. What can I do for you, George? Have you got a note for me from Betty? She seemed a bit funny in the pub.

George doesn't move. Isobel crosses to stand beside him. She glances at Wilma and takes a deep breath.

ISOBEL We want to get married, Uncle Alec.

Nothing happens for a long time. Alec seems frozen in the second before Isobel spoke. Then he looks to Wilma. Then to Smiler. Neither offers any help.

ALEC You want to get married? You want to get married? You want to get married? To each other?

They nod.

Why?

ISOBEL We're in love.

ALEC In love?

GEORGE Yes.

ALEC The Kraken Wakes! How do you know?

ISOBEL We just know.

ALEC You just know.

He turns to Wilma.

Have you ever been in love?

Wilma shakes her head.

Me neither.

He turns to Smiler.

Have you ever been in love?

SMILER With Jinty. For aboot two days.

ALEC How did you know?

SMILER I felt like I was walkin' on air. I couldnae think aboot anythin' else. I even had a bath two days runnin'. When I was with her, I thought twice about breakin' wind. I mean, I still did it, right enough, but I thought aboot it.

ISOBEL We need your blessing, Uncle Alec.

ALEC An' whit if you don't get it?

Long silence. Alec looks at Wilma.

How long is it since you got off that train in Ayr Station?

WILMA Thirteen weeks tomorrow. Why?

ALEC Fourteen weeks ago I had ma wee hoose. All to mysel'. I had ma routine. Every day was the same. I knew what was happenin' the next day, the next week, the next month. An' it was fine. It wisnae anythin' special, but it ws fine. An' I didnae have tae make decisions that involved anybody but me. But see now? I don't know if I can take much more o' this. I don't.

He leaves the room. Nobody moves much.

SMILER He's either committin' suicide or he's been taken short.

Eventually a loo flushes. Alec re-appears. They are all looking at him.

ALEC Can we agree that until the weddin', there will be no more announcements, major decisions, earthquakes, nothing?

Hugs all round. And some tears.

I feel like Galileo. No, I don't. I feel like the Pope. I feel like the Pope when Galileo came up to him an' said that black was white an' the sun moved around the earth. The Pope in Rome in fourteen-what-ever-it-was had it easy compared tae Alec Gourlay in Patna in 2011. A wee bit o' stability, eh? For God's sake. A day that starts an' ends with just gettin' older, eh? It's no' much tae ask.

SMILER I second that, so I do. Eh, Alec, by the way.

ALEC Whit?

SMILER It was the other way round. The earth an' the sun – it was the other way round.

ALEC Who cares?

The phone rings.

I'll just see who's at the door.

And he travels his own scientific path past the telephone to a door with no one on the other side.

Episode Six

INT/EXT. THE GOURLAY HOUSE. MORNING.
Alec is in his shirtsleeves, adjusting his suspenders. A bell rings. He studies the phone for a few moments, then opens the front door. A delivery boy is holding a huge and magnificent bouquet of flowers.

DELIVERY BOY Is this "Twin's Castle"?

ALEC Aye, we're waitin' for the plaque. Should've been here last week.

DELIVERY BOY Funny kinda name for a hoose.

ALEC Whit would you know aboot namin' hooses? You got some kinda Degree in it?

DELIVERY BOY I've got these flowers.

ALEC You cannae move for flowers in this hoose. Do I know you?

DELIVERY BOY I don't know.

ALEC You're no' from Patna, are you?

DELIVERY BOY Dalmellington.

ALEC Bellsbank?

DELIVERY BOY Aye.

ALEC You're no' Jimmy Milby's boy, are you?

DELIVERY BOY Aye.

ALEC Tell you what. Just give me the card, an' you take the flowers, an' put them on your father's grave.

DELIVERY BOY Ma father hated flowers.

ALEC Aye, but he's dead now, so what's the odds?

Alec takes the card and goes back inside. Wilma comes downstairs.

WILMA Who was that?

ALEC Just Smiler askin' if I fancied a quick pint, seein' as they've been open for five minutes.

WILMA You told him no, I hope.

ALEC No, actually, I said I'd join him in ten minutes or so. It's so's we can compare speeches, you see. Weed out any duplication.

WILMA We're all leaving from here. Why couldn't he have come in and done it in the living room?

ALEC You cannae move for flowers in this hoose, that's why. Cannae hear yourself think for flowers.

WILMA Are you nervous, Alec?

ALEC Of course I'm nervous. I've never done this before.

WILMA Neither have I. Nor Isobel. Nor George.

Alec is looking at the card.

ALEC Who's "Mr. Mohammed"?

WILMA Abdul. Abdul from the take-away. Did he send flowers?

ALEC Naw, just the card. It'll be their different culture, I suppose.

INT. THE "SWALLOW" PUB. MORNING.

Barbara is pulling pints for Alec and Smiler. Oswald is having trouble knotting his tie. Singer comes in.

BARBARA That'll be the three pints, then?

ALEC Singer, nae drink for you. You're drivin' the wedding car.

SINGER I know, I know. I'll just have a lemonade.

Barbara gets the drinks. Alec offers money.

BARBARA It's on the house. I can't believe you're all in here on a day like this. Anyway, we're shut for the weddin'.

ALEC It was really nice of you to come back for it, Barbara. You too, Oswald.

BARBARA George McNab gettin' married. Jinty Muir the bridesmaid. Smiler the best man. I widnae have missed it for the world. It's like somethin' oot "The Beano". Oswald's even missin' his gynaecology exam for it specially.

There are some wierd noises from upstairs.

SMILER I thought they'd have saved their chantin' for the Church.

BARBARA Here was me thinkin' you'd be savin' your wit for your speech, Smiler.

SMILER It's George McNab's speech we all cannae wait for. Hope he's remembered today's the day. Hope he's no' up the hill collectin' sheep shit for his mother's window-box.

BARBARA An' the Reception at the Burns Monument Hotel in Alloway, Alec? Bet that cost a fortune.

ALEC Nothin's too good for ma niece.

BARBARA Translated, I take it that means Wilma's payin' for everythin'?

ALEC Wilma had a wee greet this mornin'.

BARBARA I'm not surprised. Forkin' oot all that money.

ALEC [*maudlin*] It wisnae the money. It was a moment of genuine sadness. Losin' a daughter, I suppose. Losin' somebody you gave birth to.

SINGER [*perky*] Oswald. That "gynaecology". Whit's that? Whit's all that aboot?

INT. THE GOURLAY HOUSE. MORNING.
A bedroom. Wilma is doing Isobel's hair.

ISOBEL I can't believe it's not raining, Mom.

WILMA Stop fretting. It's going to be a perfect day, even if there is a change in the weather.

ISOBEL The house stinks of black pudding. Even the bedrooms. It's not going to get into my dress, is it?

WILMA Of course it won't. I've opened the windows. I did rather hope against hope Uncle Alec would forego a cooked breakfast on today of all days, but you know what he's like.

ISOBEL Where is Uncle Alec?

WILMA Comparing speeches with Smiler.

ISOBEL Is he dressed?

WILMA The full bit. You'll just have to ignore the yellow shoes. We all will. They're the only shoes he's comfortable in. He did make the effort. We spent an entire day in Ayr trying to find a black pair that fitted him, but no luck. I'll warn the photographer.

ISOBEL God, I wish it was over. The actual ceremony at least.

WILMA Why? It'll be as smooth as smooth can be.

ISOBEL I'm sure the Minister doesn't like me. He never smiles. At the rehearsal it was all he could do to make actual eye contact with George or myself. Like he didn't want to be there.

WILMA It's the limp.

ISOBEL What? I know lots of people who limp badly and still manage to be normal, friendly human beings.

WILMA It was the poodle took a lump out of his leg five years ago. Hence the muzzle. Hence the "face that would curdle milk" as Smiler puts it. And it's George's poodle. And it's you got rid of the muzzle.

The phone rings.

ISOBEL O, God! What's gone wrong? I can't bear it!

She races downstairs. Wilma sprays the room with air freshener. Isobel runs back.

WILMA Everything alright?

ISOBEL It was George.

WILMA He got the day wrong.

ISOBEL No. No, not that. He wants me to put the radio on straight away.

She fiddles with a portable machine. She finds the station. A piece of music comes to an end.

RADIO DJ That was an old 40's recording, "Tiptoe Through The Tulips", a rather unusual request, I must admit, but, as they say, it'd be a funny old world if we were all the same. And now, an even more unusual request. Not as far as the choice of music is concerned, but unusual in that it comes from Patna. Patna, for those of you lucky enough not to know it, is a ghost town half way up the Doon Valley. I don't think we've ever had a request from

Patna here on Radio Clyde. Didn't know radio had reached Patna. Sorry, Patna – only jokin'. But this is from George in Patna to his Canadian fiancee, Isobel. I don't know where you are right now, Isobel. I hope you're in Canada, not Patna. Sorry, Patna – only jokin'. But wherever you are, Isobel, this is from George in Patna to you.

> *"What A Difference A Day Made" begins to play. After a moment or two, Isobel cries tears of happiness and surprise. Before too long, Wilma joins her.*

ISOBEL Did I tell you how he proposed?

WILMA No.

ISOBEL We were up on the hill, collecting. He was his usual quiet, intent self. I was talking non-stop. It was like talking to myself, which was a good thing, because I actually was just talking to myself, just vocalising my thoughts, not to get a reply, just to sort things out in my head, I mean. I'd had the phone call that morning.

> *The song is still playing.*

ISOBEL Sacked. With a golden handshake to keep me quiet, but sacked. Jobless. What was I going to do now? What was going to happen? We sat down for a rest, me still wittering away. I thought he was playing with blades of grass, or something, out of the corner of my eye. But when I stopped for breath and looked down, he'd written "Marry me." He'd written "Marry me" In tiny balls of sheep shit.

INT. THE B & B. LATE MORNING.
Alec, Smiler and Betty are drinking tea.

ALEC You're absolutely sure George is upstairs?

BETTY Of course I'm sure. Why?

ALEC Just checkin'. Widnae want anythin' tae go wrong.

BETTY Anythin' like whit?

SMILER Like the bridegroom havin' a wee memory lapse an' bein' up the hill fillin' a bag wi' sheep shit for your window-box, instead o' exchangin' rings wi' Alec's niece.

BETTY He's upstairs havin' a bath, I tell you.

SMILER It must be love, right enough, then.

ALEC It's funny tae think, isn't it, that here he is, lyin' in a bath in Patna, an' tomorrow night he'll be thousands o' miles away in Canada on his honeymoon.

BETTY He's never been further than Edinburgh.

ALEC Has he ever flown before?

SMILER Did you hear what Betty just said? Edinburgh. How could he ever have flown before?

ALEC It's ma nerves, Smiler. I'm no' thinkin straight.

Betty pours more tea for everyone.

SMILER Do you realise that in two hours' time you two'll be related?

ALEC Means nothin'.

SMILER Of course it means things.

ALEC Like whit?

SMILER Like you cannae shag if you're related.

BETTY Smiler Fulton! Stop that filthy talk at once!

SMILER Just tryin' tae be helpful. Everybody gets frisky at weddins. An' I always thought Alec had a wee glint for you.

BETTY I'll not tolerate talk like that in ma hoose!

SMILER Aye, fair enough. But you've got [*consults his watch*] one hour forty minutes if you change your minds.

ALEC How's Eddie these days, Betty?

BETTY In a world of his own somewhere. He seems a wee bit more at peace these last two or three months. I went over tae the Nursing Home yesterday. I don't think he recognises even me. He's well enough in body. It's just his mind's gone. Five years he's been in that place. That Home. It just came like a bolt oot the blue, the senility. One minute he was fine, the next, he'd lost it. Makes you think, eh? It's just as well we don't know what's in store for us, eh? Whit's round the next corner.

ALEC Aye, livin' for the moment's the answer, right enough.

SMILER One hour thirty eight an' a half minutes.

INT. THE "SWALLOW" PUB. EARLY AFTERNOON.

The pub is empty and quiet. Singer enters from the toilet area with a gynaecology textbook.

SINGER Very interesting, Oswald. Opened ma eyes tae a few things. You hivnae got another one wi' pictures in it, have you?

He realises there is no one there. At least not in the bar. He wonders about the rest of the building.

He returns to the Gents and glances round. On the wall someone has written, "Alistair Loves Maureen. True For Ever". He checks the cubicles. They're empty.

Gingerly, he knocks on the door of the Ladies. There's no response. He goes in. On the wall someone has written, "Maureen Loves Stewart. True For Ever." These cubicles are empty as well.

He climbs the stairs tentatively. There is a series of photographs on the wall. All of Bob and Ida Hyslop at various religious gatherings. Like shaking hands with the Moderator of the General Assembly of the Church of Scotland.

He reaches a bedroom door and knocks. He waits, then pushes it open. Ladies make-up is scattered untidily. There's a photo of Barbara and Oswald on the dressing-table, and a textbook lying on the single bed. He opens it. Advanced Mathematics. He closes it.

The second bedroom, which he enters after knocking, is tidy. A suitcase on the floor. Another textbook. This one is on Gynaecology. He browses, but there are no pictures.

He knocks on the third bedroom door, waits, pushes it open. Above the bed is the Hyslops' wedding photograph. The room is an Aladdin's Cave of sex aids. The lot. You name it. The double bed is covered in an assortment of whips.

The phone rings. He finds it and answers.

SINGER Hello? ... Aye, it's Singer ... Whit am I doin' here? I'm answerin' the phone. Is that you, Alec? How's it goin'? ... Do I know whit time it is? Aye, [*consults a clock*] it's exactly ten past one ... O, aye, the weddin'. Pick youse up for the weddin' ... Aye, sure enough, I'll be there straight away, Alec. Two minutes ... I was in the toilet ... There's no need tae swear like that ... Aye ... Cheerio, then.

He goes back downstairs to leave. The door is locked. He tries a window. It's locked. He looks out. He sighs, and goes back upstairs. He finds a phone book, searches for a number, finds it and dials.

... Alec? ... Aye, it's me ... Mobile?

He moves the phone around.

Well, it's mobile, but it's not *a* mobile, if you see what I mean ... I'm still in the pub ... Because I think they're all at the Church, an' they've locked me in ... Well, there's actually not a lotta point breakin' a window, Alec, because the other thing is that when I looked oot, I notice I've forgotten tae pick up the weddin' car, it's still in Dalmellington ... Alec?

He replaces the receiver and sits and thinks.

He goes back down to the bar. He looks around, shrugs, pulls himself a pint. He drinks some of it, then switches on the dart-board light. He rests his pint on the window sill and throws three darts.

One hundred and eighty!!

INT/EXT. THE GOURLAY HOUSE. EARLY AFTER-NOON.

Alec slams the phone down. Gathered round him are Wilma, Isobel, Smiler and Jinty.

ALEC The bampot! I hope he gets haemorrhoids like grapes an' his collection of Jim Reeves CD's catches fire!

WILMA Shall we telephone for a taxi?

ALEC The nearest rank's in Dalmellington. We're gonnae have tae walk. I cannot believe that man!

SMILER [*to Isobel*] If I was younger, I'd give you a piggy-back, hen.

ISOBEL I'll be fine, Smiler.

SMILER A day to remember, right enough.

ALEC Let's go.

Everybody troops outside. Alec closes the door.

Did I turn the gas off?

WILMA Don't you dare go back in there, Alec Gourlay! We're already fifteen minutes late.

A bus turns the corner and stops.

BUS DRIVER [*calling out*] You're never goin' tae a weddin' in they shoes, are you?

ALEC Don't you bother your heid aboot ma shoes. How's about doin' somethin' useful for a change an' drivin' us up tae the Church?

BUS DRIVER It's no' on ma route.

ALEC Bugger your route! There'll be naebody in Patna wantin' your stupid bus anyway! They're all up at the Church. How's about it, eh?

BUS DRIVER Ma bus is no' stupid!

ALEC Alright, your bus is no' stupid, but how's about it, eh?

BUS DRIVER Aye, well, jump in. That's a few tins o' spaghetti hoops you owe me.

They all clamber aboard, past the Sales Assistant and the Lingerie Assistant, who are sitting near the front. The Sales Assistant turns round.

SALES ASSISTANT Fear not. You're in good hands. That's ma man drivin'.

She suddenly spots Alec and Smiler.

Hey! I recognise youse!

She prods the Lingerie Assistant.

Look, Mary! That's they two auld fellas who came intae the shop a coupla months ago tae buy a bra!

They fall about laughing. Alec and Smiler are mortified.

LINGERIE ASSISTANT Aye, so it is! We had the whole shop in stitches wi' that story. He says he's lookin' at the bras, an' I says whit size, an' he shrugs, an' the other one says is she aboot Jinty's size, an' he says maybe a wee bit bigger, an' the other one – him there – he holds up his hand like this, like he was holdin' a wee melon or a grapefruit, an' says, this size, hen.

They find it hilarious, oblivious to Jinty's mortification.

BUS DRIVER Here we are, then. I think this'll be the Church, right enough.

The bus stops by the crowds at the Church. The Minister limps towards it. The wedding party scramble off and head for the Church entrance. A man comes up to the bus door.

MAN Is this the Ayr bus?

BUS DRIVER Aye, jump in.

MAN You're no' goin' through Dalrymple, are you?

BUS DRIVER Naw.

MAN That's alright, then.

The man jumps on. The bus pulls away. As it turns the corner, a sheep ambles onto the road. The driver accelerates.

BUS DRIVER Venison, here we come!

INT. BURNS MONUMENT HOTEL. LATE AFTERNOON.

The central area of a large room is clear for dancing. Guests are on the side tables, finishing their meal. At the top table, left to right, are the Minister, Betty, Wilma, Isobel, George, Alec, Jinty and Smiler.

JINTY [*to Smiler*] I was black affronted on that bus, so I was.

ALEC It's a compliment that he remembered, Jinty. You should feel flattered. An' I have tae say, you're lookin' great today. Like somethin' oot a catalogue. I bet the weddin' photos are goin' to be stupendous.

JINTY As long as the photographer cuts your shoes off.

Smiler looks around.

SMILER I think everybody's finished eatin' now, Alec. Except Tam the postman. "Can I have a side-order of chips wi' ma dessert?" You couldnae take him anywhere.

ALEC Everybody seems tae be enjoyin' themselves, that's the main thing.

SMILER Betty's givin' that champagne laldy. Her glass is never empty. It'll dae her bowels the world o' good, mind you.

JINTY Do we have tae talk aboot bowels on an occasion like this?

SMILER Some folks' lives are ruled by their bowels, Jinty. There's nae point in brushin' them under the carpet.

ALEC Tam's wipin' his mooth, so I suppose this is as good a moment as any.

He taps his glass with a knife for silence and gets to his feet.

Ladies an' Gentlemen, a wee bit o' wheesh, if you don't mind.

He brings out a speech which he reads straight. Nothing improvised, no trying for laughs.

First of all, I'd like tae thank youse all for comin' today to the weddin' of ma niece, Isobel, tae George McNab. An' thank youse for all the lovely presents youse gave the young couple. It was very kind of youse, and they will be treasured forever as momentos of this very special day. I know some of youse haven't given presents yet because it slipped your mind, but when you do deliver them to Wilma and me, we'll put them in storage in Ayr if they're big enough, until the newly-weds return from their Canadian honeymoon, even though there'll be a bit of expense involved. But on a day like this, that's bye the bye. Next, it's ma duty to thank Mr. Mackintosh of the Burns Monument Hotel and his wonderful staff for the splendid meal an' the excellent service. An' talkin' about service, a word of thanks tae the Minister for keepin' it short, simple, an' to the point. There are some folk I wish could have been here today tae see all this happenin'. Smiler's parents, who brought me up. Ma mother, who left me on Smiler's doorstep when I was four. Ma father, whoever he was. It would have been nice tae see them here, but they're all dead, an' that's life. It would be wrong of me if I didnae give special mention tae Wilma, the bride's mother, for payin' for all this, an' for bein' ma sister, an' for turnin' ma world upside doon, but not so as anythin' fell an' broke. My one remainin' duty, as the nearest thing tae a father the bride has got, is to ask you all tae be upstanding an' raise your glasses tae the bride an' groom. Ladies an' Gentlemen, I give you – the bride an' groom!

The couple are toasted, and Alec applauded. George rises. You could hear a pin drop. George speaks without notes.

GEORGE I'm aware it's suddenly gone as quiet as the grave, an' I know fine why. None of you have ever heard me talk for more than fifteen seconds at the one time, an' you're expectin' me tae make an arse o' this, an' I'm gonnae try an' disappoint you. I've grown up wi' the reputation of bein' the village idiot, an' I'm not sayin' I don't deserve that, but maybe I didnae have much tae say tae folk, maybe I kept a lot inside, even kept it from counsellors an' doctors they sent me tae. When ma father went into the Home, ma mother turned the hoose intae a Bed an' Breakfast place. She put new covers on the sofa, an' a lock on the bathroom door. She got worm tablets for the dog, an' new curtains. She got pens done that said, "McNab's Bed And Breakfast", an' had the flags of all the EEC countries on them. She put adverts in tourist magazines. That was five years ago. Naebody came. Naebody phoned. Naebody knocked on the door. Until a few months ago, when I was up the hill collectin' sheep shit for ma mother's window-box. That was Isobel. I'm sorry tae say this, Minister, but I don't know if there is a God. I really don't. If there is, I widnae thank him for whit he's done tae ma father. I widnae thank him for whit he did tae the miners. But I would thank him for Isobel. I'm not that silly that I don't know how lucky I am. Ladies an' Gentlemen, I give you – ma wife.

They toast Isobel. George sits to prolonged and loud applause and a big kiss from Isobel. There are quite a few hankies out. Smiler rises.

SMILER Aye, very good. It was alright, that, George. It wisnae Peter Ustinov, but it was alright. Now, as best man, I'm here tae propose a toast tae Jinty Muir, the bridesmaid. Who looks radiant today, I must say. Lovely frock, lovely skin. Even though she didnae eat her vegetables, or any o' the melon or grapefruit we had for starters. But before we toast Jinty, there's a coupla other things I have tae say.

He takes out a small slip of paper.

Mr. Mackintosh, the manager here, has asked me tae point out that the contraceptive vending machine in the Gents toilet isnae workin'. An' seein' as this is the first time since the miners' strike that nearly the whole o' Patna is in the same room, Andy Park from Dalmellington asked me tae say that the Silver Band there is short of cornet players. Doctor Macdonald asked me tae remind youse that under no circumstances will he look at what's wrong wi' your pets, so don't bother bringin' them tae the surgery. An' the bus company want me tae let you know, that as from next Monday, the four o'clock bus tae Ayr is goin' direct, an' will not be goin' through Dalrymple. For which news, much thanks.

Applause and cheers.

Ladies an' Gentlemen – I give you the bridesmaid!

Jinty is toasted and applauded.

An' now I'd like the bride an' groom to lead off the dancin', the first one bein', in honour of Alec's twin sister, a Canadian Barn Dance!

Isobel and George are the first couple on the floor, followed by Alec and Betty, then Wilma and the Minister, then Jinty and Smiler, and eventually other guests until the dance floor is packed. The dance ends to applause.

ACCORDIANIST An' the next dance is an Excuse Me waltz!

Lots of couples get up. Alec partners Isobel. Wilma waltzes with Smiler. The Hyslop parents dance together. Abdul taps Smiler on the shoulder and takes his place with Wilma.

ABDUL [*dancing*] I hope the flowers were O.K, Miss Gourlay. I chose them myself.

Elsewhere Singer taps Bob Hyslop's shoulder to partner his wife. As they waltz –

SINGER Thanks for comin' back an' lettin' me oot, Mrs. Hyslop.

IDA Nae problem. When we set off, we didnae know you were still in the toilet.

They're dancing.

SINGER I think the weather's on the turn.

IDA At least it's stayed dry for the weddin'.

SINGER Aye, but I went out for a breath of fresh air a coupla minutes ago, an' the wind's fair gettin' up.

IDA Is it?

SINGER Aye, it's fair *whippin'* through the trees. It was *whippin'* round ma ankles. Aye, fair *whippin'* , it was.

EXT. AYR RAILWAY STATION. MORNING.
Isobel and George are leaning out of a window of the train which is about to depart. Wilma, Alec, Betty and Smiler are on the platform.

BETTY I wish that engine was quieter. Ma head's beelin'.

SMILER It's all that champagne, Betty. That's whit's caused the hangover. You were knockin' it back like there was no tomorrow. At least it gave you the runs as well. Every cloud has a silver lining, as they say. It's an ill wind, an' all that.

WILMA You will telephone the minute you get there, won't you?

ISOBEL I promise, Mom.

GEORGE [*to Betty*] Are you gonna be alright?

BETTY I'll get a bus back as soon as the train's went.

WILMA Don't worry, George, I'll make sure she's alright.

The Guard blows his whistle.

I guess this is it, then.

ISOBEL Thanks for everything, Mom. And you, Uncle Alec. And you, Mrs. McNab ... Mom. You too, Smiler.

SMILER It was a pleasure. Think nothin' of it. Whit are you thankin' me for?

The train begins to move.

ISOBEL Love you!

WILMA Love you!

ALEC Love you!

> *Maybe he's never said this before. Everybody waves until the train is out of sight.*

SMILER [*to Alec*] Did you clock the driver?

ALEC [*wiping his eyes*] Naw. Why?

SMILER Never mind Canada, they'll be lucky if they get tae Glasgow. He was wearin' an Ayr United scarf.

EXT. AYR SEA FRONT. MORNING.

> *Alec and Smiler are walking. A little boy is playing cowboys on his own. He has two toy guns. His mother is a little way off.*

SMILER Are you fast wi' them?

LITTLE BOY Aye.

SMILER Bet you're no' as fast as me.

LITTLE BOY Bet I am.

SMILER We'll find out, shall we?

> *He takes one of the guns and sticks it in his belt.*

On the count of three, alright?

> *The little boy nods.*

One! Two! Three!

> *They both draw and shout "bang!".*

I won. Told you I would.

LITTLE BOY You didnae win!

SMILER I did so!

LITTLE BOY Did not! I was faster! You're deid!

SMILER I'm no'! You're deid! I won!

LITTLE BOY Didnae!

SMILER Did!

The little boy's mother has arrived. She takes the gun off Smiler.

MOTHER I think it was equal. You're both just as fast as each other. I think we should call it a draw.

SMILER It wisnae a draw! I beat him!

MOTHER He's only four!

SMILER I don't care whit age he is! I beat him!

The mother comforts her son, leading him away. Alec and Smiler walk on in silence. The gulls are swooping. A plane flies overhead. You can just about make out the island of Arran through the mist.

I beat him, didn't I, Alec?

ALEC Aye. Aye, you beat him, Smiler.

Lightning Source UK Ltd.
Milton Keynes UK
UKOW04f0708281214

243634UK00001B/73/P